COGNITIVE BEHAVIORAL THERAPY (CBT)

2 Manuscripts
Introducing Cognitive Behavioral Therapy, Cognitive Behavioral Therapy Made Simple

Examples and techniques you can use in your daily life.

Introducing

COGNITIVE BEHAVIORAL THERAPY

By

Daniel Anderson

TABLE OF CONTENTS

CHAPTER ONE

TAKING COGNIZANCE OF THE COMMON MENTAL HEALTH ISSUES

Anxiety

Feeling worried or nervous is a normal part of everyday life. Everyone frets or feels anxious from time to time. Mild to moderate anxiety can help you focus your attention, energy, and motivation. If anxiety is severe, you may have feelings of helplessness, confusion, and extreme worry that are out of proportion with the actual seriousness or likelihood of the feared event. Overwhelming anxiety that interferes with daily life is not normal. This type of anxiety may be a symptom of generalized anxiety disorder, or it may be a symptom of another problem, such as depression.

Jane's story

"Jane has always been a worrier, but it never interfered with her life before. Lately, however, she's been feeling keyed up all the time. She's paralyzed by an omnipresent sense of dread, and worries constantly about the future. Her worries make it difficult to concentrate at work, and when she gets home she can't relax. Jane is also having sleep difficulties, tossing and turning for hours before she falls asleep. She also gets frequent stomach cramps and diarrhea, and has a chronic stiff neck from muscle tension. Jane feels like she's on the verge of a nervous breakdown."

What is GAD?

Everyone gets worried sometimes, but if you have generalized anxiety disorder (GAD),it is overwhelming and can dominate one's day with inappropriate and exaggerated worries and tension, even when there is nothing present to worry about. GAD is often accompanied by physical symptoms or sensations like a racing heart, breathlessness, nausea, can't sleep,chest pains and sweating for example.

Generalized anxiety disorder (GAD) involves anxiety and worry that is excessive and unrelenting. This high-level anxiety makes normal life difficult and relaxation impossible. If you have generalized anxiety disorder (GAD) you may worry about the same things that other people do: health issues, money, family problems, or difficulties at work. But you take these worries to a new level.

Normal worry vs. Generalized Anxiety Disorder (GAD)

Normal'Worry:

• Your worrying doesn't get in the way of your daily activities and responsibilities.

• You're able to control your worrying.

•Your worries, while unpleasant, don't cause significant distress.

• Your worries are limited to a specific, small number of realistic concerns.

• Your bouts of worrying last for only a short time period.

Generalized Anxiety Disorder:

• Your worrying significantly disrupts your job, activities, or social life.

• Your worrying is uncontrollable.

• Your worries are extremely upsetting and stressful.

• You worry about all sorts of things, and tend to expect the worst.

• You've been worrying almost every day for at least six months.

GAD sufferers seem unable to eliminate or ignore their concerns, even though they usually realize that their anxiety is more intense than the situation warrants.

GAD sufferers may often feel light-headed or out of breath. They may also feel nauseated or have to go to the bathroom frequently. Generalized anxiety is constant and can cause anxiety/panic attacks during the day and night. Night time anxiety and panic attacks are especially disturbing and can often wake the sufferer from deep sleep feeling particularly frightened. Night time anxiety can be minimized with some practical steps which minimize the impact of such things as blood sugar level fluctuations during sleep.

Individuals with GAD seem unable to relax, and they may startle more easily than other people. They tend to have difficulty concentrating and often, they have trouble falling or staying asleep.

The sort of symptoms you can experience in generalized anxiety are generally milder than those experienced during an anxiety / panic attack. Although distressing, they are usually much less extreme but may include some of the symptoms outlined on our anxiety symptoms list.

Your stomach may churn, your heart races or beats slower or you may get palpitations you may also feel sweaty or clammy, dizzy or shaky and general unrest.

You may just feel as if you have the Flu with shaky or weak legs and clamminess. You might get disturbing thoughts or feel depressed, this is perfectly normal and will pass, it is purely a response to anxiety and must not be mistaken for depression. Remember, these thoughts and feelings are harmless but unpleasant none the less.

So let us look some levels of anxiety, such as: "Mum there's a great big spider in my bedroom" cries a child and the child gets anxious about the spider, a specific creature she imagines can hurt her. Anxiety always relates to hurt. This is a controllable anxiety, get rid of the spider equals getting rid of the anxiety, (carefully looking to see there are no other spiders lurking there). I would call this third-line-anxiety. A learned anxiety, overcome with reason and action. This anxiety is a learned one, where the growing person has learned that certain things can harm us and being little (in psyche if not body) there is a need for immediate help from others perceived as being stronger than the self. This is usually enough and can be used in a creative and useful manner. An example would be learning self-defence to ward off bullies at school. There is also the chronic worrier who perceives their worry as an anxiety state, and rightly so, we may say anxiety at a lesser level. I would call this second-line anxiety. Overcome with specific understanding of the self. This is also reasonably easy to overcome by getting to know who you really are. This is not as hard as you may think.

However there is also another anxiety, of varying degrees, one where it 'takes over' the emotions and won't go away. A terrifying emptiness of blackness filled with 'spiders' of our deep inner psyche's creation, not simply one in the bedroom that can be overcome by a bit of reason, muscle and mum's trusty broom. I would call this first-line anxiety. This is often very difficult to clear, not because it can't be cleared, but by the very nature of distrust on which all anxiety is founded. Anxiety is a very real but unconscious form of expression of the hurting child

Let's understand where anxiety comes from. This may be a bit heavy, but stay in there and you'll be supplied with information you need to give you a foundation of knowledge to underpin your new, productive actions. You see, all life must express itself in its own way. You are special part of that life and you have been since you were first united as one by the penetration of daddy's sperm into mummy's egg. The life then created was a NEW and powerful life. Very different to the first two living creatures (egg and sperm) and already eager to get stuck into life into mummy's womb where it forms into another new life (life meeting life again). Then you grow into a baby, and all the experiences of mother as she carries you are recorded in your little psyche. Then you are born. What an experience! Life (baby) meeting life (the world baby will live in).

Here is how it ideally works:

Essentially the growing baby wants mother's attentions at all times. Baby has already gone through the amazing life series of development of all the organs of the body and has broken from being dependent on the mother, has travelled the sometimes very scary birth canal and is eager to go on to new things. All this at an emotional level. Then baby goes through a series of transitional developments... firstly the need for acceptance. This is the prime essential and we all carry that through life to the grave. From acceptance baby moves to Being. A genuine, real little bundle of life that has father as a guarantee of strength and mother as an assurance of sustenance, both vital to the growing child. Then with mother and father there to sustain life as a right, baby moves to what can be called Wellbeing. From there on to Identification where baby identifies with mother to gain his personal identity and from father for his social identity. Further development for the well-parented child leads to Status as a person and then on to Production.

But what if there is a blockage somewhere along that ideal chain? What if mother does NOT come when called upon by baby's very real needs? What would happen if the normal cycle was BLOCKED, for whatever reason, at the first stage when mother was NOT there to supply her loving acceptance/ sustenance? The inner pain can be endured for a time, but then baby may feel that mother will never come and a panic starts to become a pathway within the developing psyche. This pathway has no name as it's an indefinable feeling,but it's REAL to baby and it starts to develop its own pathways within the psyche. There starts a despair, a hopelessness and the ability to wait for the second stage of BEING by mother's coming is weakened. Infantile death! Baby doesn't know this of course, and it's all pushed into the feeling unconscious to be drawn on at any time later in life when similar experiences are presented.

Here is the foundation of hopelessness, the substance for anxiety.

Let me give you an illustration:

A lady came to me with a terrible anxiety about money. She was single, attractive, intelligent. Money was a terrifying agent for her anxiety on a large scale, permeating all she did. However her older brother was a millionaire by age 21! Same parents, same parental love shared by both. Both accepted. What was the difference? It appeared that her father was a very successful businessman in a middle eastern country. His livelihood was taken away from him by an antagonistic government action. The very lives of the father, mother and son were seriously at risk so they fled to United States as immigrants with absolutely no money at all. The mother was devastated at all this and my client was conceived during this calamitous period. She wore her mother's grief (loss of livelihood) mother's desperation (lack of money) mother's shame (social scorn) and now mother's contribution to poverty (becoming pregnant) In US, the father resumed his business talents and again became wealthy, the son following dad's social example, but the girl only knew, among all the love shared in the family, the distress that associated with money. The son felt prosperity. That was HIS inner picture. The girll felt poverty-anxiety. THAT was her inner picture. She was able to step out of that state with the adult mind of CHOICE leaving behind the anxiety-feeling mind of the inner CHILD.

I will show you how you can do that also a little later.

At each stage of acceptance, being, wellbeing, identification, status, productivity, varying degrees of blocking can take place, leaving behind it's legacy of anxiety. Here is first line trauma. Bearing in mind that we are a complex of genetics, ego strength, ancestral and cellular memories, and family dynamics so it would be difficult indeed for a therapist to get to the bottom of it all.

So let's look at the basics of anxiety and as we go, if you feel (note the word feel) something stirring within you, take note of it, maybe write it down for your attention later on.

WE are a complex of many ingredients and all of these ingredients and circumstances join together to make the strength of our ego (who we believe ourselves to be). If a person has a strong ego they will act accordingly and if a weak ego (or none at all) they will act accordingly. Makes sense. But for the growing child the sense of power lies in the parenting, especially mother. So the little ego will react to the bad as well as the good in it's own strength. This is why you are unique. No one is the same as you and YOU have the inner answer to your inner anxiety.

Let's look at how it can operate:

Baby can, and does, suffer from mental anguish at the loss of BEING through the loss of mother's attentions, for whatever reason, (don't go blaming mum as it quite often, indeed almost always, someone else messing up her routine with baby) and this results in dread sometimes with rage attached and sometimes beyond rage with depressions as a result. Different babies, different ego-responses. What happens in this case is baby develops a feeling, nay, a TERROR of the death of the spirit. Baby (you and me) has been through.

The joys and energetic drives of LIFE! LIVING! Taking LIFE as LIFE itself with all of the energetic joys of getting 'stuck into life' in mother's endometrium. BLISS! And now being denied this feeling of LIFE! and an emerging sense of DEATH!

This once LIFE! Being somehow blocked and this blocking taking away that BEING so essential to baby's growth - a growth that cannot be stopped except by death. So: delusional fears of death (self or close persons). Being preoccupied with impending death. Doom. Disaster. Hell. So with this mind-set there is an entry into a panic state, intense apprehension, ANXIETY as a first-line anxiety.

A sense of despair 'takes over'. Various phobias are revealed that are peculiar to the experiences of the little baby/child. The ability to wait for 'the good' to come in the form of some accepting person is almost nil. The BEING is challenged by a feeling of separation that will never be satisfied. Therefore no sustenance. A hopelessness called anxiety. This feeling was once REAL and the feeling is still REAL to the inflicted person. However note that it is a FEELING and as such cannot harm you in any way. A harmless but intense feeling that simply 'takes over' as it did when baby was experiencing the FACT of non-BEING.

Anxiety at this level can lead to endless talking about their terrible plight. Feeling 'locked in' to endless bad relationships. Difficult to maintain true friendships, which fuels the anxiety. Shutting one's self off from help. Isolated by others. More anxiety.

Indeed there are so many paths that can be developed by the human psyche regarding anxiety we could wonder if there is ANY real, basic relief from it's malevolent attacks. Let's look at some of the expressions of this malady, remembering that if baby was caught in this terrifying experience the deepest REPRESSION covers this desperate infantile deprivation and can lead to the death of the spirit in dread. It is a basic TERROR.

Caught in a RAGE Catch 22: Not to rage as a baby/child is to die by isolation. To rage is to both destroy and be destroyed. Have you had that feeling? If so, this is your story. Anxiety releases infantile RAGE and dreams (nightmares?) of how to destroy the whole rotten anxiety mess. The mother delay becomes an intolerable bondage, forced into the unconscious, but wanting to DO something (fright, flight, fight) which translates into the physical counterparts of: tense head feelings, buzzing in the ears, head throbbing, nose often congested, vision blurred, tight chest, breathing irregular, heart beating fast, blood pressure up, loss of appetite, nervous dyspepsia, tight stomach, constipated, loss of weight, muscles tight and aching, pains in the neck and limbs, tremors, fidgeting, sweating, blotchy skin, menstruation preceded by tension, irritable, angry scenes, sexual libido often lost, and there are others. Survival is therefore by fight as mounting rage is an attempt to force a response. This is all an active aggressive response to this separation-anxiety.

Or we may go into the phobic areas of expression of our anxiety. there is only one anxiety, but many expressions of it: Agoraphobia, Claustrophobia, Fears of loss of consciousness, Hospitals, Separation, Being sick. etc.

Attention seeking can become a fixation with infantile dependent behaviour attached.

Any usual output is thereby lost, the energies being put to the inner world of the child within, unconsciously fighting from a platform of dire distress. Weakness or tiredness takes over. Not wanting to either start or finish a task.

Fatigue can become persistent and quite strong.

Loss of concentration. Can't read and remember what has been read. Little if any concern for others. Small problems become major events. Easily distracted. Antisocial. Not a party-goer. Only partial attempts to become party to activities.

Moods are gloomy with heavy, stony grief. Irritable, whining, always lamenting. All the good times are in the past. Memory selects past grievances. All is experienced as painful, even any happy times, and can't feel love for family or show or feel real grief.

Depersonalised and incapable of emotion. Unreality feelings include being 'outside myself' or 'not there'. Time drags. Colours look drab, or all is seen as grey.

The spirits are low, especially in the morning o after sleep. Negative people, Denies inner hostility. God is seen as distant, angry and rejecting.

As personalities before the trigger of anxiety in this level is activated, they could well have been well adjusted and outgoing. Others cold have been dependent and anxious with a record of hard work, anxiously, meticulously and over-conscientiously performed.

In this case they would have been denied mother, as a baby, but also had attentions not of their satisfaction, as a surrogate mother, or nurse. So you can see that there could be many variants and only YOU would have that, unconsciously, in your psyche.

Anxiety can cause physical and emotional symptoms. A specific situation or fear can cause some or all of these symptoms for a short time. When the situation passes, the symptoms usually go away.

Physical symptoms of anxiety include:

• Trembling, twitching, or shaking.

• Feeling of fullness in the throat or chest.

- Breathlessness or rapid heartbeat.

- Light-headedness or dizziness.

- Sweating or cold, clammy hands.

- Feeling jumpy.

- Muscle tension, aches, or soreness (myalgias).

- Extreme tiredness.

Sleep problems, such as the inability to fall asleep or stay asleep, early waking, or restlessness (not feeling rested when you wake up).

Anxiety affects the part of the brain that helps control how you communicate. This makes it harder to express yourself creatively or function effectively in relationships. Emotional symptoms of anxiety include:

- Restlessness, irritability, or feeling on edge or keyed up.

- Worrying too much.

- Fearing that something bad is going to happen; feeling doomed.

- Inability to concentrate; feeling like your mind goes blank.

Anxiety disorders

Anxiety disorders occur when people have both physical and emotional symptoms. Anxiety disorders interfere with how a person gets along with others and affect daily activities. Women are twice as likely as men to have problems with anxiety disorders. Examples of anxiety disorders include panic attacks, phobias, and generalized anxiety disorder.

Often the cause of anxiety disorders is not known. Many people with an anxiety disorder say they have felt nervous and anxious all their lives. This problem can occur at any age. Children who have at least one parent with the diagnosis of depression are more likely to have an anxiety disorder than other children.

Anxiety disorders often occur with other problems, such as:

Mental health problems, such as depression.

Substance use problems.

A physical problem, such as heart or lung disease. A complete medical examination may be needed before an anxiety disorder can be diagnosed.

Panic attacks

A panic attack is a sudden feeling of extreme anxiety or intense fear without a clear cause or when there is no danger. Panic attacks are common. They sometimes occur in otherwise healthy people. An attack starts suddenly and usually lasts from 5 to 20 minutes but may last even longer. You have the most anxiety about 10 minutes after the attack starts.

Symptoms include feelings of dying or losing control of yourself, rapid breathing (hyperventilation), numbness or tingling of the hands or lips, and a racing heart. You may feel dizzy, sweaty, or shaky. Other symptoms include trouble breathing, chest pain or tightness, and an irregular heartbeat. These symptoms come on suddenly and without warning.

Sometimes symptoms of a panic attack are so intense that the person fears he or she is having a heart attack. Many of the symptoms of a panic attack can occur with other illnesses, such as hyperthyroidism, coronary artery disease, or chronic obstructive pulmonary disease (COPD). A complete medical examination may be needed before an anxiety disorder can be diagnosed.

People who have repeated unexpected panic attacks and worry about the attacks are said to have a panic disorder.

Depression

While everyone feels sad from time to time, major depression is very different. Major depressive disorder or clinical depression causes you to experience feelings of sadness, loneliness, or a loss of interest in things you once enjoyed. When these feelings occur for more than two weeks, doctors may diagnose this as major depressive disorder. These symptoms are a sign that you need to seek professional help. Talk to your doctor if you have symptoms that may indicate depression.

Common symptoms of depression

Symptoms of depression can vary. They may manifest themselves differently from person to person. However, for most people, depression symptoms affect their ability to perform daily activities, interact with others, or go to work or go to school. If you suffer from depression you may often experience several of the following:

Sadness

The most common symptom of depression is a feeling of sadness or emptiness that lasts for more than two weeks. A person may describe this symptom as a feeling of "hopelessness." They may feel as if life will not get better and that this intense level of sadness will last forever. If this feeling lasts longer than two years it's known as dysthymia. This is a type of chronic depression in which a person's moods are consistently low.

Worthlessness

Continual feelings of worthlessness, guilt, or helplessness often accompany the condition. People tend to focus on personal shortcomings or past failures. They often blame themselves when their life isn't going the way they would like. Teenagers who experience depression commonly report feelings of worthlessness. They may report feeling misunderstood and start to avoid interactions with others.

Irritability

Depression may cause people to get easily frustrated or angered, even over small or insignificant matters. This often relates back to a person experiencing levels of tension and fatigue that makes it difficult to get through the day. Men and women may display irritability symptoms differently from each other. Women often report feeling angry at one moment, and then tearful at the next. Men may appear volatile or aggressive due to their depression. Traditional male roles in society may also mean that a man displays irritability for not being able to "get it together" and overcome depressive symptoms.

Fatigue

People with depression often experience lack of energy or feel tired all the time. Small tasks, like showering or getting out of bed, may seem to require more effort than one can muster. Fatigue can play a role in other symptoms associated with depression, such as withdrawal and apathy. You may feel overwhelmed at the mere thought of exertion or going outdoors.

Guilt

Depression is often the result of imbalanced chemicals in the brain. However, people experiencing depression may blame themselves for their symptoms instead. Statements such as "I can't do anything right" or "everything is my fault," become the norm for you.

Crying spells

People who have depression may find themselves crying frequently for no apparent reason. Crying spells can be a symptom of post-partum depression, which can occur in a woman after she's given birth.

Apathy

People with depression commonly lose interest or stop finding pleasure in activities that they once enjoyed, including sex.

Anxiety

Anxiety is a feeling of impending doom or danger, even when there isn't a justifiable reason. Depression can cause a person to feel anxious all the time. A person may say they are constantly tense, but there's no direct threat or identifiable source for this tension.

Restlessness

Agitation and restlessness, including pacing, an inability to sit still, or hand wringing, may occur with depression.

Lack of concentration

People with depression may have a difficult time remembering, maintaining focus, or making decisions. Fatigue, feelings of worthlessness, or feeling "numb" can turn decision-making into a talk that is difficult to accomplish. Friends or family members may discuss specific dates or events, but you may not remember just moments later due to concentrating lack of concentration. This inability to concentrate can lead to withdrawal in a depressed person.

Withdrawal

Many people with depression shut themselves off from the world. They may isolate themselves, not answer the phone, or refuse to go out with friends. You feel as if you're "numb," and that nothing will bring you joy.

Sleep problems

People's sleep habits are likely to change as a result of depression. They may not be able to fall asleep or stay asleep. They may wake up in the middle of the night and not go back to sleep at all. You may sleep for long periods and find that you don't want to get out of bed. These symptoms lead to fatigue that can exacerbate additional symptoms of depression, such as a lack of concentration.

Overeating or loss of appetite

Depression can often cause a lack of interest in food and weight loss. In other people, depression leads to overeating and weight gain. This is because a person may feel so frustrated or miserable that they turn to food as a means to escape their problems. However, overeating can lead to weight gain and cause you to exhibit low levels of energy. Not enough food can also cause you to also have low energy levels and feel weak.

Thoughts of suicide

Thinking or fantasizing about death is a serious sign that needs to be addressed right away. According to the Mayo Clinic, thoughts of suicide are symptoms common in older men. Loved ones may not initially notice this thinking and pass a person's depression symptoms off as age-related mental health changes. However, depression and especially suicidal thoughts are never normal emotions.

If you or a loved one is thinking of hurting themselves, seek immediate medical attention. At the emergency room, a doctor can help you get mental health care until these feelings subside.

Physical pain

Physical symptoms, such as body pain, headaches, cramps, and digestive problems also can occur. Younger children with depression commonly report physical pain symptoms. They may refuse to go to school or behave particularly clingy due to the worry about their aches and pains.

Phobias

Fear is a powerful and primitive human emotion. It alerts us to the presence of danger and it was critical in keeping our ancestors alive. Fear can be divided into two responses, biochemical and emotional. The biochemical response is universal, while the emotional response is highly individual.

Biochemical Reaction

Fear is a natural emotion and a survival mechanism. When we confront a perceived threat, our bodies respond in specific ways. Physical reactions to fear include sweating, increased heart rate, and high adrenaline levels that make us extremely alert. This physical response is also known as the "fight or flight" response, in which your body prepares itself to either enter combat or run away. This biochemical reaction is likely an evolutionary development. It's an automatic response that is crucial to our survival.

Emotional Response

The emotional response to fear is highly personalized. Because fear involves some of the same chemical responses in our brains that positive emotions like happiness and excitement do, feeling fear under certain circumstances can be seen as fun, like when you watch scary movies. Some people are adrenaline junkies, thriving on extreme sports and other fear-inducing thrill situations. Others have a negative reaction to the feeling of fear, avoiding fear-inducing situations at all costs. Although the physical reaction is the same, fear may be perceived as either positive or negative, depending on the person.

Causes of Fear

Fear is incredibly complex. Some fears may be a result of experiences or trauma, while others may actually represent a fear of something else entirely, such as a loss of control. Still other fears may occur because they cause physical symptoms, such as being afraid of heights because they make you feel dizzy and sick to your stomach, even if you're simply watching a video or looking at a picture and in no actual danger.

Scientists are trying to understand exactly what fear is and what causes it, but this is a supremely difficult undertaking in light of the differences between individuals in terms of what they fear and why. Not to mention that there is no agreement between scientists who study fear as to whether it's a sort of behavior that's only observable or something our brains are physically wired to do.

Fear is the basis of anxiety but it is not the only anxiety attack symptom. Treatment for your anxiety needs to address this fear first, however, because it is the trigger for anxiety.

You'll likely want to look at natural anxiety relief, rather than drug-induced treatments because at some point, you will want to be drug and anxiety free.

So let's talk about fear itself and how you can start treating yourself now.

Where does this fear come from? Why does it cause such distress and feed anxiety as well as it does? What can you do to stop it?

There have been many theories around fear and its role as an anxiety attack symptom. Treatment options are equally diverse. Some are scams while others have proven to be highly effective, regardless of how long you've suffered anxiety attack symptoms.

Having suffered years of anxiety, I underwent the related medical treatments. The medications merely kept me calm while I went through 3 years of therapy, but when it was over, the fear had eased but it hadn't gone away.

Then one day, I discovered the secret behind that fear. Today, I immediately recognize when the fear is stirring and can halt it immediately.

If you can identify your fear, you will be able to do the same.

First let me say that I disagree with the approach that you don't have to know what causes the fear, and that it's only important to know that the fear is simply an anxiety attack symptom. For me, it was imperative I figure out the fear so I could deal with it. And when I did, my anxiety attacks subsided.

I hope this secret I'm about to reveal helps you too.

The first thing to realize is that fear comes from your subconscious. Your body senses a danger or perceived danger and responds with fear. Fear causes your body to increase its adrenalin so it can fight to preserve itself. Today, however, much of the fear is internalized rather than from an outside source, like a threat from a wild animal.

It's true that over time our experiences have taught us to respond automatically with this fear instinct. When it gets out of control, as when it becomes an anxiety attack symptom, treatment must be sought.

Let's start with your thoughts, because that's where the fear hides.

If you listen closely when you feel an anxiety attack coming on, you'll get a sense that something just happened to scare you. You know that feeling you get when you go into a room and forget why you went there? Fear as an anxiety attack symptom feels much the same. Inside, you feel uncomfortable. It's a feeling that's difficult to pinpoint or explain. You just sense something isn't right.

I firmly believe that the fear builds because now you are afraid of the fear itself, just as popular programs say. You don't understand where it's coming from and this makes you believe something terrible is going to happen.

This 'something' that caused your unease might be a memory your subconscious has suppressed. For instance, let's say you had a bad experience years ago when you had to go to a meeting. Perhaps you were asked to make a brief presentation, but you hadn't been notified in advance and weren't prepared. You immediately felt fear. This is a natural response to such an unexpected event.

One day, you're going about your business and something reminds you of that nerve-wracking event and the fear you felt resurfaces, but you try to suppress it. This time, you can't pinpoint what's causing it. You have now set up an automatic fear response that will continue until you find a way to deal with it.

When you sense your fear, stop and think about what just happened. What were you thinking about? Are you anxious about something in your life? Often, we have day-to-day 'fears' about things. We worry over finances, health, career, family, retirement, an expected move.

Perhaps you're having trouble meeting your bill payments. Maybe you have to do something you don't particularly feel comfortable doing. Maybe you are going somewhere and you're nervous about the trip for some reason.

Take time to sit down and write out the things that make you nervous, fearful, stressed. Cover your personal traits - for example, if you're a homebody and would rather keep to yourself than attend a meeting or go to a social gathering. Include any traumatic events in your life, going right back to the beginning.

Have you lost loved ones recently? Are you concerned about your life without them? This is particularly tough and might require help from bereavement support groups. Be sure to take advantage of them, because they can provide tremendous help in moving on.

How's your self esteem? Do you feel good about yourself? You might have to really think critically to discover just who you are and why you are the way you are. Write it all down and see if you can identify the things that trigger your fear.

See, my occasional lack of confidence will make me uncertain when I have to take on certain tasks. I'm not sure I can handle them, or that I'll do a good job. Now I know this is a threat to my self-esteem. If I fail, it shows I'm not as good as I'd like to believe.

Failing only reveals my weaknesses and limitations. Because self-esteem is necessary to live comfortably, fear results from this 'threat'. And yes, that fear can soon turn into an anxiety attack if I don't take those few minutes to catch those fleeting thoughts that caused it.

First you need to work on fear - your anxiety attack symptom. Treatment begins at home, as they say.

I've discovered that just the act of halting my fear to stop and think about what just went through my mind was enough to bring the anxiety attack to an end in a matter of seconds. As soon as that happened, I was able to think about the fear and focus on solutions, rather than on the fear itself.

Have you ever wakened from a dream and immediately forgotten what it was, but it felt important to remember? You struggled to recall it so you could find out what happened or resolve the problem. Think of your fear as a dream - something in your subconscious that you can resolve.

Remember too, that most fear is fear of the unknown. Identify your fear and it no longer has control over you. You have control over it, and your anxiety.

I wish I could better explain this process, but the best I can advise is to watch your thinking. Listen to yourself, to your thoughts. Understand who you are. Take the time to sit down and truly evaluate what makes you tick.

Be honest in your personal evaluation. It can be difficult, but it's absolutely necessary for this to work. Often we don't recognize how we think, especially when we're talking about the subconscious. For instance, you might believe you have good self esteem and that you're upbeat and forward-thinking. You can be almost certain this is not entirely true in all situations. Ask your partner or family member for feedback if necessary. Sometimes an outside source can pick up things you'll miss.

Acclimation

Repeated exposure to similar situations leads to familiarity. This greatly reduces both the fear response and the resulting elation, leading adrenaline junkies to seek out ever new and bigger thrills. It also forms the basis of some phobia treatments, which depend on slowly minimizing the fear response by making it feel familiar.

Psychology of Phobias

One aspect of anxiety disorders can be a tendency to develop a fear of fear. Where most people tend to experience fear only during a situation that is perceived as scary or threatening, those who suffer from anxiety disorders may become afraid that they will experience a fear response. They perceive their fear responses as negative and go out of their way to avoid those responses.

A phobia is a twisting of the normal fear response. The fear is directed toward an object or situation that does not present a real danger. Though you recognize that the fear is unreasonable, you can't help the reaction. Over time, the fear tends to worsen as the fear of fear response takes hold.

CHAPTER TWO

BECOME FAMILIAR WITH THE BASIC PRINCIPLES OF CBT AND UNDERSTAND HOW IT WORKS

The History Of Cognitive Behavioral Therapy

Cognitive behavioral therapy is an approach used by psychotherapists to influence a patient's behaviors and emotions. The key to the approach is in its procedure which must be systematic. It has been used successfully to treat a variety of disorders including eating disorders, substance abuse, anxiety and personality disorders. It can be used in individual or group therapy sessions and the approach can also be geared towards self help therapy.

Cognitive behavioral therapy is a combination of traditional behavioral therapy and cognitive therapy. They are combined into a treatment that is focused on symptom removal. The effectiveness of the treatment can clearly be judged based on its results. The more it is used, the more it has become recommended. It is now used as the number one treatment technique for post traumatic stress disorder, obsessive compulsive disorder, depression and bulimia.

Cognitive behavioral therapy first began to be used between 1960 and 1970. It was a gradual process of merging behavioral therapy techniques and cognitive therapy techniques. Behavioral therapy had been around since the 1920's, but cognitive therapy was not introduced until the 1960's. Almost immediately the benefits of combining it with behavioral therapy techniques were realized. Ivan Pavlov, with his dogs who salivated at the ringing of the dinner bell, was among the most famous of the behavioral research pioneers. Other leaders in the field included John Watson and Clark Hull.

Instead of focusing on analyzing the problem like Freud and the psychoanalysts, cognitive behavioral therapy focused on eliminating the symptoms. The idea being that if you eliminate the symptoms, you have eliminated the problem. This more direct approach was seen as more effective at getting to the problem at hand and helping patients to make progress more quickly.

As a more radical aggressive treatment, behavioral techniques dealt better with more radical problems. The more obvious and clear cut the symptoms were, the easier it was to target them and devise treatments to eliminate them. Behavioral therapy was not as successful initially with more ambiguous problems such as depression. This realm was better served with cognitive therapy techniques.

In many academic settings, the two therapy techniques were used side by side to compare and contrast the results. It was not long before the advantages of combining the two techniques became clear as a way of taking advantage of the strengths of each. David Barlow's work on panic disorder treatments provided the first concrete example of the success of the combined strategies.

Cognitive behavioral therapy is difficult to define in a succinct definition because it covers such a broad range of topics and techniques. It is really an umbrella definition for individual treatments that are specifically tailored to the problems of a specific patient. So the problem dictates the specifics of the treatment, but there are some common themes and techniques. These include having the patient keep a diary of important events and record the feelings and behaviors they had in association with each event. This tool is then used as a basis to analyze and test the patient's ability to evaluate the situation and develop an appropriate emotional response. Negative emotions and behaviors are identified as well as the evaluations and beliefs that lead to them. An effort is then made to counter these beliefs and evaluations to show that the resulting behaviors are wrong. Negative behaviors are eliminated and the patient is taught a better way to view and react to the situation.

Part of the therapy also includes teaching the patient ways to distract themselves or change their focus from something that is upsetting or a situation that is generating negative behavior. They learn to focus on something else instead of the negative stimulus, thus eliminating the negative behavior that it would lead to. The problem is essentially nipped in the bud. For serious psychological disorders like bipolar disorder or schizophrenia, mood stabilizing medications are often prescribed to use in conjunction with these techniques. The medications give the patient enough of a calming effect to give them the opportunity to examine the situation and make the healthy choice whereas before they could not even pause for rational thought.

Cognitive behavioral therapy has been proven effective for a variety of problems, but it is still a process, not a miracle cure. It takes time to teach patients to understand situations and identify the triggers of their negative behaviors. Once this step is mastered, it still takes a lot of effort to overcome their first instincts and instead stop and make the right choices. First they learn what they should do, and then they must practice until they can do it.

The Basics of Cognitive Behavioral Therapy

The underlying concept behind CBT is that our thoughts and feelings play a fundamental role in our behavior. For example, a person who spends a lot of time thinking about plane crashes, runway accidents and other air disasters may find themselves avoiding air travel.

The goal of cognitive behavior therapy is to teach patients that while they cannot control every aspect of the world around them, they can take control of how they interpret and deal with things in their environment.

Cognitive behavior therapy has become increasingly popular in recent years with both mental health consumers and treatment professionals. Because CBT is usually a short-term treatment option, it is often more affordable than some other types of therapy. CBT is also empirically supported and has been shown to effectively help patients overcome a wide variety of maladaptive behaviors.

Cognitive behavioral therapy is a psychotherapeutic approach that aims to teach a person new skills on how to solve problems concerning dysfunctional emotions, behaviors, and cognitions through a goal-oriented, systematic approach. This title is used in many ways to differentiate behavioral therapy, cognitive therapy, and therapy that is based on both behavioral and cognitive therapies. There is empirical evidence that shows that cognitive behavioral therapy is quite effective in treating several conditions, including personality, anxiety, mood, eating, substance abuse, and psychotic disorders. Treatment is often manualized, as specific psychological orders are treated with specific technique-driven brief, direct, and time-limited treatments.

Cognitive behavioral therapy can be used both with individuals and in groups. The techniques are often adapted for self-help sessions as well. It is up to the individual clinician or researcher on whether he/she is more cognitive oriented, more behavioral oriented, or a combination of both, as all three methods are used today. Cognitive behavioral therapy was born out of a combination of behavioral therapy and cognitive therapy. These two therapies have many differences, but found common ground on focusing on the "here and now" and on alleviating symptoms.

Evaluating cognitive behavioral therapy has led to many believing that it is more effective over psychodynamic treatments and other methods. The United Kingdom advocates the use of cognitive behavioral therapy over other methods for many mental health difficulties, including post-traumatic stress disorder, obsessive-compulsive disorder, bulimia nervosa, clinical depression, and the neurological condition chronic fatigue syndrome/myalgic encephalomyelitis. The precursors of cognitive behavioral therapy base their roots in various ancient philosophical traditions, especially Stoicism. The modern roots of CBT can be traced to the development of behavioral therapy in the 1920s, the development of cognitive therapy in the 1960s, and the subsequent merging of the two therapies. The first behavioral therapeutic approaches were published in 1924 by Mary Cover Jones, whose work dealt with the unlearning of fears in children.

The early behavioral approaches worked well with many of the neurotic disorders, but not so much with depression. Behavioral therapy was also losing in popularity due to the "cognitive revolution." This eventually led to cognitive therapy being founded by Aaron T. Beck in the 1960s. The first form of cognitive behavioral therapy was developed by Arnold A. Lazarus during the time period of the late 1950s through the 1970s. During the 1980s and 1990s, cognitive and behavioral therapies were combined by work done by David M. Clark in the United Kingdom and David H. Barlow in the United States. Cognitive behavioral therapy includes the following systems: cognitive therapy, rational emotive behavior therapy, and multimodal therapy. One of the greatest challenges is defining exactly what a cognitive-behavioral therapy is. The particular therapeutic techniques vary within the different approaches of

CBT depending upon what kind of problem issues are being dealt with, but the techniques usually center around the following:

- Keeping a diary of significant events and associated feelings, thoughts, and behaviors.

- Questioning and testing cognitions, evaluations, assumptions, and beliefs that might be unrealistic and unhelpful.

- Gradually facing activities that may have been avoided.

- Trying out new ways of behaving and reacting.

In addition, distraction techniques, mindfulness, and relaxation are also commonly used in cognitive behavioral therapy. Mood-stabilizing medications are also often combined with therapies to treat conditions like bipolar disorder. The NICE guidelines within the British NHS recognize cognitive behavioral therapy's application in treating schizophrenia in combination with medication and therapy. Cognitive behavioral therapy usually takes time for patients to effectively implement it into their lives. It usually takes concentrated effort for them to replace a dysfunctional cognitive-affective-behavioral process or habit with a more reasonable and adaptive one, even when they recognize when and where their mental processes go awry. Cognitive behavioral therapy is applied to many different situations, including the following conditions:

Anxiety disorders (obsessive-compulsive disorder, social phobia or social anxiety, generalized anxiety disorder)

Mood disorders (clinical depression, major depressive disorder, psychiatric symptoms)

Insomnia (including being more effective than the drug Zopiclone)

Severe mental disorders (schizophrenia, bipolar disorder, severe depression)

Children and adolescents (major depressive disorder, anxiety disorders, trauma and posttraumatic stress disorder symptoms)

Stuttering (to help them overcome anxiety, avoidance behaviors, and negative thoughts about themselves)

Cognitive behavioral therapy involves teaching a person new skills to overcome dysfunctional emotions, behaviors, and cognitions through a goal-oriented, systematic approach. There is empirical evidence showing that cognitive behavioral therapy is effective in treating many conditions, including obsessive-compulsive disorder, generalized anxiety disorder, major depressive disorder, schizophrenia, anxiety, and negative thoughts about oneself). With the vast amount of success shown by the use of this therapy, it is one of the most important tools that researchers and therapists have to treat mental disorders today.

Automatic Negative Thoughts

One of the main focuses of cognitive-behavioral therapy is on changing the automatic negative thoughts that can contribute to and exacerbate emotional difficulties, depression, and anxiety. These negative thoughts spring forward spontaneously, are accepted as true, and tend to negatively influence the individual's mood.

Through the CBT process, patients examine these thoughts and are encouraged to look at evidence from reality that either supports or refutes these thoughts. By doing this, people are able to take a more objective and realistic look at the thoughts that contribute to their feelings of anxiety and depression. By becoming aware of the negative and often unrealistic thoughts that dampen their feelings and moods, people are able to start engaging in healthier thinking patterns.

Types of Cognitive Behavior Therapy

According to the British Association of Behavioural and Cognitive Psychotherapies, "Cognitive and behavioral psychotherapies are a range of therapies based on concepts and principles derived from psychological models of human emotion and behavior. They include a wide range of treatment approaches for emotional disorders, along a continuum from structured individual psychotherapy to self-help material."

There are a number of specific types of therapeutic approaches that involve CBT that are regularly used by mental health professionals. Examples of these include:

Rational Emotive Behavior Therapy (REBT): This type of CBT is centered on identifying and altering irrational beliefs. The process of REBT involves identifying the underlying irrational beliefs, actively challenging these beliefs, and finally learning to recognize and change these thought patterns.

Cognitive Therapy: This form of therapy is centered on identifying and changing inaccurate or distorted thinking patterns, emotional responses, and behaviors.

Multimodal Therapy: This form of CBT suggests that psychological issues must be treated by addressing seven different but interconnected modalities, which are behavior, affect, sensation, imagery, cognition, interpersonal factors and drug/biological conside-rations.

Dialectical Behavior Therapy: This type of cognitive-behavioral therapy addresses thinking patterns and behaviors and incorporates strategies such as emotional regulation and mindfulness.

While each type of cognitive-behavioral therapy offers its own unique approach, each centers on addressing the underlying thought patterns that contribute to psychological distress.

The Components of Cognitive Behavior Therapy

People often experience thoughts or feelings that reinforce or compound faulty beliefs. Such beliefs can result in problematic behaviors that can affect numerous life areas, including family, romantic relationships, work, and academics.

For example, a person suffering from low self-esteem might experience negative thoughts about his or her own abilities or appearance. As a result of these negative thinking patterns, the individual might start avoiding social situations or pass up opportunities for advancement at work or at school.

In order to combat these destructive thoughts and behaviors, a cognitive-behavioral therapist begins by helping the client to identify the problematic beliefs. This stage, known as functional analysis, is important for learning how thoughts, feelings, and situations can contribute to maladaptive behaviors. The process can be difficult, especially for patients who struggle with introspection, but it can ultimately lead to self-discovery and insights that are an essential part of the treatment process.

The second part of cognitive behavior therapy focuses on the actual behaviors that are contributing to the problem. The client begins to learn and practice new skills that can then be put in to use in real-world situations. For example, a person suffering from drug addiction might start practicing new coping skills and rehearsing ways to avoid or deal with social situations that could potentially trigger a relapse.

In most cases, CBT is a gradual process that helps a person take incremental steps towards a behavior change. Someone suffering from social anxiety might start by simply imagining himself in an anxiety-provoking social situation.

Next, the client might start practicing conversations with friends, family, and acquaintances. By progressively working toward a larger goal, the process seems less daunting and the goals easier to achieve.

The Process of Cognitive Behavior Therapy

During the process of CBT, the therapist tends to take a very active role.

CBT is highly goal-oriented and focused, and the client and therapist work together as collaborators toward the mutually established goals.

The therapist will typically explain the process in detail and the client will often be given homework to complete between sessions.

Cognitive-behavior therapy can be effectively used as a short-term treatment centered on helping the client deal with a very specific problem.

Uses of Cognitive Behavior Therapy

Cognitive behavior therapy has been used to treat people suffering from a wide range of disorders, including:

1. Anxiety

2. Phobias

3. Depression

4. Addictions

5. Eating disorders

6. Panic attacks

7. Anger

CBT is one of the most researched types of therapy, in part because treatment is focused on highly specific goals and results can be measured relatively easily.

Compared to psychoanalytic types of psychotherapy which encourage a more open-ended self-exploration, cognitive behavior therapy is often best-suited for clients who are more comfortable with a structured and focused approach in which the therapist often takes an instructional role. However, for CBT to be effective, the individual must be ready and willing to spend time and effort analyzing his or her thoughts and feelings. Such self-analysis and homework can be difficult, but it is a great way to learn more about how internal states impact outward behavior.

Cognitive behavior therapy is also well-suited for people looking for a short-term treatment option for certain types of emotional distress that does not necessarily involve psychotropic medication. One of the greatest benefits of cognitive-behavior therapy is that it helps clients develop coping skills that can be useful both now and in the future.

Although therapy must be tailored to the individual, there are, nevertheless, certain principles that underlie cognitive behavior therapy for all patients. I will use a depressed patient, "Amy," to illustrate these central tenets and to demonstrate how to use cognitive theory to understand patients' difficulties and how to use this understanding to plan treatment and conduct therapy sessions.

Amy was an 18-year-old single female when she sought treatment with me during her second semester of college. She had been feeling quite depressed and anxious for the previous 4 months and was having difficulty with her daily activities. She met criteria for a major depressive episode of moderate severity according to DSM-IV-TR (the Diagnostic and Statistical Manual of Mental Disorders, Fourth Edition, Text Revision; American Psychiatric Association, 2000). The basic principles of cognitive behavior therapy are as follows:

Principle No. 1: Cognitive behavior therapy is based on an ever-evolving formulation of patients' problems and an individual conceptualization of each patient in cognitive terms. I consider Amy's difficulties in three time frames. From the beginning, I identify her current thinking that contributes to her feelings of sadness ("I'm a failure, I can't do anything right, I'll never be happy"), and her problematic behaviors (isolating herself, spending a great deal of unproductive time in her room, avoiding asking for help). These problematic behaviors both flow from and in turn reinforce Amy's dysfunctional thinking.

Second, I identify precipitating factors that influenced Amy's perceptions at the onset of her depression(e.g., being away from home for the first time and struggling in her studies contributed to her belief that she was incompetent).

Third, I hypothesize about key developmental events and her enduring patterns of interpreting these events that may have predisposed her to depression (e.g., Amy has had a lifelong tendency to attribute personal strengths and achievement to luck, but views her weaknesses as a reflection of her "true" self).

I base my conceptualization of Amy on the cognitive formulation of depression and on the data Amy provides at the evaluation session. I continue to refine this conceptualization at each session as I obtain more data. At strategic points, I share the conceptualization with Amy to ensure that it "rings true" to her. Moreover, throughout therapy I help Amy view her experience through the cognitive model. She learns, for example, to identify the thoughts associated with her distressing affect and to evaluate and formulate more adaptive responses to her thinking. Doing so improves how she feels and often leads to her behaving in a more functional way.

Principle No. 2: Cognitive behavior therapy requires a sound therapeutic alliance. Amy, like many patients with uncomplicated depression and anxiety disorders, has little difficulty trusting and working with me. I strive to demonstrate all the basic ingredients necessary in a counseling situation: warmth, empathy, caring, genuine regard, and competence. I show my regard for Amy by making empathic statements, listening closely and carefully, and accurately summarizing her thoughts and feelings. I point out her small and larger successes and maintain a realistically optimistic and upbeat outlook. I also ask Amy for feedback at the end of each session to ensure that she feels understood and positive about the session.

Principle No. 3: Cognitive behavior therapy emphasizes collaboration and active participation. I encourage Amy to view therapy as teamwork; together we decide what to work on each session, how often we should meet, and what Amy can do between sessions for therapy homework. At first, I am more active in suggesting a direction for therapy sessions and in summarizing what we've discussed during a session. As Amy becomes less depressed and more socialized into treatment, I encourage her to become increasingly active in the therapy session: deciding which problems to talk about, identifying the distortions in her thinking, summarizing important points, and devising homework assignments.

Principle No. 4: Cognitive behavior therapy is goal oriented and problem focused. I ask Amy in our first session to enumerate her problems and set specific goals so both she and I have a shared understanding of what she is working toward. For example, Amy mentions in the evaluation session that she feels isolated. With my guidance, Amy states a goal in behavioral terms: to initiate new friendships and spend more time with current friends. Later, when discussing how to improve her day-to-day routine, I help her evaluate and respond to thoughts that interfere with her goal, such as: My friends won't want to hang out with me. I'm too tired to go out with them. First, I help Amy evaluate the validity of her thoughtsthrough an examination of the evidence. Then Amy is willing to test the thoughts more directly through behavioral experiments in which she initiates plans with friends. Once she recognizes and corrects the distortion in her thinking, Amy is able to benefit from straightforward problem solving to decrease her isolation.

Principle No. 5: Cognitive behavior therapy initially emphasizes the present. The treatment of most patients involves a strong focus on current problems and on specific situations that are distressing to them. Amy begins to feel better once she is able to respond to her negative thinking and take steps to improve her life. Therapy starts with an examination of here-and-now problems, regardless of diagnosis. Attention shifts to the past in two circumstances: One, when patients express a strong preference to do so, and a failure to do so could endanger the therapeutic alliance. Two, when patients get "stuck" in their dysfunctional thinking, and an understanding of the childhood roots of their beliefs can potentially help them modify their rigid ideas. ("Well, no wonder you still believe you're incompetent. Can you see how almost any child—who had the same experiences as you—would grow up believing she was incompetent, and yet it might not be true, or certainly not completely true?")

For example, I briefly turn to the past midway through treatment to help Amy identify a set of beliefs she learned as a child: "If I achieve highly, it means I'm worthwhile," and "If I don't achieve highly, it means I'm a failure." I help her evaluate the validity of these beliefs both in the past and present. Doing so leads Amy, in part, to develop more functional and more reasonable beliefs. If Amy had had a personality disorder, I would have spent proportionally more time discussing her developmental history and childhood origin of beliefs and coping behaviors.

Principle No. 6: Cognitive behavior therapy is educative, aims to teach the patient to be her own therapist, and emphasizes relapse prevention. In our first session I educate Amy about the nature and course of her disorder, about the process of cognitive behavior therapy, and about the cognitive model (i.e., how her thoughts influence her emotions and behavior). I not only help Amy set goals, identify and evaluate thoughts and beliefs, and plan behavioral change, but I also teach her how to do so. At each session I ensure that Amy takes home therapy notes— important ideas she has learned—so she can benefit from her new understanding in the ensuing weeks and after treatment ends.

Principle No. 7: Cognitive behavior therapy aims to be time limited. Many straightforward patients with depression and anxiety disorders are treated for six to 14 sessions. Therapists' goals are to provide symptom relief, facilitate a remission of the disorder, help patients resolve their most pressing problems, and teach them skills to avoid relapse. Amy initially has weekly therapy sessions. (Had her depression been more severe or had she been suicidal, I may have arranged more frequent sessions.) After 2 months, we collaboratively decide to experiment with biweekly sessions, then with monthly sessions. Even after termination, we plan periodic "booster" sessions every 3 months for a year. Not all patients make enough progress in just a few months, however. Some patients require 1 or 2 years of therapy (or possibly longer) to modify very rigid dysfunctional beliefs and patterns of behavior that contribute to their chronic distress. Other patients with severe mental illness may need periodic treatment for a very long time to maintain stabilization.

Principle No. 8: Cognitive behavior therapy sessions are structured. No matter what the diagnosis or stage of treatment, following a certain structure in each session maximizes efficiency and effectiveness. This structure includes an introductory part (doing a mood check, briefly reviewing the week, collaboratively setting an agenda for the session), a middle part (reviewing homework, discussing problems on the agenda, setting new homework, summarizing), and a final part (eliciting feedback). Following this format makes the process of therapy more understandable to patients and increases the likelihood that they will be able to do self-therapy after termination.

Principle No. 9: Cognitive behavior therapy teaches patients to identify, evaluate, and respond to their dysfunctional thoughts and beliefs. Patients can have many dozens or even hundreds of automatic thoughts a day that affect their mood, behavior, or physiology (the last is especially pertinent to anxiety). Therapists help patients identify key cognitions and adopt more realistic, adaptive perspectives, which leads patients to feel better emotionally, behave more functionally, or decrease their physiological arousal. They do so through the process of guided discovery, using questioning (often labeled or mislabeled as "Socratic questioning") to evaluate their thinking (rather than persuasion, debate, or lecturing). Therapists also create experiences, called behavioral experiments, for patients to directly test their thinking (e.g., "If I even look at a picture of a spider, I'll get so anxious I won't be able to think"). In these ways, therapists engage in collaborative empiricism. Therapists do not generally know in advance to what degree a patient's automatic thought is valid or invalid, but together they test the patient's thinking to develop more helpful and accurate responses.

When Amy was quite depressed, she had many automatic thoughts throughout the day, some of which she spontaneously reported and others that I elicited (by asking her what was going through her mind when she felt upset or acted in a dysfunctional manner). We often uncovered important automatic thoughts as we were discussing one of Amy's specific problems, and together we investigated their validity and utility. I asked her to summarize her new viewpoints, and we recorded them in writing so that she could read these adaptive responses throughout the week to prepare her for these or similar automatic thoughts. I did not encourage her to uncritically adopt a more positive viewpoint, challenge the validity of her automatic thoughts, or try to convince her that her thinking was unrealistically pessimistic. Instead we engaged in a collaborative exploration of the evidence.

Principle No. 10: Cognitive behavior therapy uses a variety of techniques to change thinking, mood, and behavior. Although cognitive strategies such as Socratic questioning and guided discovery are central to cognitive behavior therapy, behavioral and problem-solving techniques are essential, as are techniques from other orientations that are implemented within a cognitive framework. For example, I used Gestalt-inspired techniques to help

Amy understand how experiences with her family contributed to the development of her belief that she was incompetent. I use psychodynamically inspired techniques with some Axis II patients who apply their distorted ideas about people to the therapeutic relationship. The types of techniques you select will be influenced by your conceptualization of the patient, the problem you are discussing, and your objectives for the session.

These basic principles apply to all patients. Therapy does, however, vary considerably according to individual patients, the nature of their difficulties, and their stage of life, as well as their developmental and intellectual level, gender, and cultural background. Treatment also varies depending on patients' goals, their ability to form a strong therapeutic bond, their motivation to change, their previous experience with therapy, and their preferences for treatment, among other factors. The emphasis in treatment also depends on the patient's particular disorder(s). Cognitive behavior therapy for panic disorder involves testing the patient's catastrophic misinterpretations (usually life- or sanity-threatening erroneous predictions) of bodily or mental sensations. Anorexia requires a modification of beliefs about personal worth and control. Substance abuse treatment focuses on negative beliefs about the self and facilitating or permission-granting beliefs about substance use.

How does it work?

Cognitive behavioural therapy (CBT) can help you make sense of overwhelming problems by breaking them down into smaller parts.

Some forms of psychotherapy focus on looking into the past to gain an understanding of current feelings. In contrast, CBT focuses on present thoughts and beliefs.

CBT can help people with many problems where thoughts and beliefs are critical. It emphasizes the need to identify, challenge, and change how a person views a situation.

According to CBT, people's pattern of thinking is like wearing a pair of glasses that makes us see the world in a specific way. CBT makes us more aware of how these thought patterns create our reality and determine how we behave.

In CBT, problems are broken down into five main areas:

• situations

• thoughts

• emotions

• physical feelings

• actions

CBT is based on the concept of these five areas being interconnected and affecting each other. For example, your thoughts about a certain situation can often affect how you feel both physically and emotionally, as well as how you act in response.

How CBT is different

CBT differs from many other psychotherapies because it's:

Pragmatic – it helps identify specific problems and tries to solve them

Highly structured – rather than talking freely about your life, you and your therapist discuss specific problems and set goals for you to achieve

Focused on current problems – it's mainly concerned with how you think and act now rather than attempting to resolve past issues

Collaborative – your therapist won't tell you what to do; they'll work with you to find solutions to your current difficulties

Stopping negative thought cycles

There are helpful and unhelpful ways of reacting to a situation, often determined by how you think about them.

For example, if your marriage has ended in divorce, you might think you've failed and that you're not capable of having another meaningful relationship.

This could lead to you feeling hopeless, lonely, depressed and tired, so you stop going out and meeting new people. You become trapped in a negative cycle, sitting at home alone and feeling bad about yourself.

But rather than accepting this way of thinking you could accept that many marriages end, learn from your mistakes and move on, and feel optimistic about the future.

This optimism could result in you becoming more socially active and you may start evening classes and develop a new circle of friends.

This is a simplified example, but it illustrates how certain thoughts, feelings, physical sensations and actions can trap you in a negative cycle and even create new situations that make you feel worse about yourself.

CBT aims to stop negative cycles such as these by breaking down things that make you feel bad, anxious or scared. By making your problems more manageable, CBT can help you change your negative thought patterns and improve the way you feel.

CBT can help you get to a point where you can achieve this on your own and tackle problems without the help of a therapist.

Exposure therapy

Exposure therapy is a form of CBT particularly useful for people with phobias or obsessive compulsive disorder (OCD).

In such cases, talking about the situation isn't as helpful and you may need to learn to face your fears in a methodical and structured way through exposure therapy.

Exposure therapy involves starting with items and situations that cause anxiety, but anxiety that you feel able to tolerate. You need to stay in this situation for one to two hours or until the anxiety reduces for a prolonged period by a half.

Your therapist will ask you to repeat this exposure exercise three times a day. After the first few times, you'll find your anxiety doesn't climb as high and doesn't last as long.

You'll then be ready to move to a more difficult situation. This process should be continued until you have tackled all the items and situations you want to conquer.

Exposure therapy may involve spending six to 15

hours with the therapist, or can be carried out using self-help books or computer programs. You'll need to regularly practice the exercises as prescribed to overcome your problems.

CBT sessions

CBT can be carried out with a therapist in one-to-one sessions or in groups with other people in a similar situation to you.

If you have CBT on an individual basis, you'll usually meet with a CBT therapist for between five and 20 weekly or fortnightly sessions, with each session lasting 30-60 minutes.

Exposure therapy sessions usually last longer to ensure your anxiety reduces during the session. The therapy may take place:

In a clinic

Outside – if you have specific fears there

In your own home – particularly if you have agoraphobia or OCD involving a specific fear of items at home

Your CBT therapist can be any healthcare professional who has been specially trained in CBT, such as a psychiatrist, psychologist, mental health nurse or GP.

First sessions

The first few sessions will be spent making sure CBT is the right therapy for you, and that you're comfortable with the process. The therapist will ask questions about your life and background.

If you're anxious or depressed, the therapist will ask whether it interferes with your family, work and social life. They'll also ask about events that may be related to your problems, treatments you've had, and what you would like to achieve through therapy.

If CBT seems appropriate, the therapist will let you know what to expect from a course of treatment. If it's not appropriate, or you don't feel comfortable with it, they can recommend alternative treatments.

Further sessions

After the initial assessment period, you'll start working with your therapist to break down problems into their separate parts. To help with this, your therapist may ask you to keep a diary or write down your thought and behaviour patterns.

You and your therapist will analyse your thoughts, feelings and behaviours to work out if they're unrealistic or unhelpful and to determine the effect they have on each other and on you. Your therapist will be able to help you work out how to change unhelpful thoughts and behaviours.

After working out what you can change, your therapist will ask you to practise these changes in your daily life.

This may involve:

Questioning upsetting thoughts and replacing them with more helpful ones

Recognizing when you're going to do something that will make you feel worse and instead doing something more helpful

You may be asked to do some "homework" between sessions to help with this process.

At each session, you'll discuss with your therapist how you've got on with putting the changes into practice and what it felt like. Your therapist will be able to make other suggestions to help you.

Confronting fears and anxieties can be very difficult. Your therapist won't ask you to do things you don't want to do and will only work at a pace you're comfortable with. During your sessions, your therapist will check you're comfortable with the progress you're making.

One of the biggest benefits of CBT is that after your course has finished, you can continue to apply the principles learned to your daily life. This should make it less likely that your symptoms will return.

CHAPTER THREE

HOW TO DEFINE A SPECIFIC GOAL TO WORK TOWARD OVER THE COURSE OF 6 WEEKS

Because of CBT's success, some of its tenants have become well-known. You might already have heard, for example, that thoughts affect feelings, or that behavioural change can affect negative thoughts.

But what other Cognitive Behavioral Therapy techniques and tools are there, and how do they help you? How are these CBT techniques used in a session?

AGENDA SETTING IN CBT

This is a collaborative process between your therapist and you to determine how to best make use of each session. At the start of each appointment both you and your therapist suggest items you'd like to discuss. A decision is then made on the order the points will be discussed, and how much time each one needs.

The point of agenda setting is to make sure that the session is well spent, and that the hour isn't lost to something that isn't of itself productive, like simply rehashing the events of the week. It is always a good idea to be thinking before your session about what you want to put on the agenda, so you don't walk away feeling something important was missed.

In the first few sessions your therapist will model for you how to set agendas. So you don't have to instantly feel comfortable enough to add items to the agenda yourself, but can learn over time. This is itself a valuable process, helping you take charge of your problems and their solutions.

GOAL-SETTING IN CBT

Again, this is a collaborative process designed to maintain structure and focus. The point is to make the goals for your therapy those that are relevant to you, with input from your therapist to make sure they are clear and are what you actually want as opposed to what you think you should want. Goal-setting makes CBT productive by highlighting the possibility of change, making insurmountable problems appear more manageable, and increasing your hope of overcoming them.

While there are many different approaches to goal setting, one of the more common techniques used by CBT therapists is the SMART way.

SMART goal setting creates a clear and vivid picture of your goal and helps you maintain your motivation for achieving it.

This is what the acronym stands for :

Specific: Avoid generalisation. Be clear and focused

on exactly what you want. A specific goal has a much greater chance of being accomplished than a general goal.

Measurable: Establish concrete criteria for measuring progress toward the attainment of each goal you set. Ask yourself questions such as, "How much?" and "How many?" "How will I know when I have met my goal?"

Achievable: Make your goals attainable and feasible! How are you going to make this goal a reality? What can you do to make it more achievable?

Realistic: Is your goal realistic given your skills, time frame, etc? While setting high goals can be a great way of increasing motivation, it can also be disheartening when they are so high that you cannot reach them. This can leave you feeling like a failure.

Timely: Set realistic time-frames to avoid procrastination or giving up on your goal.

In pursuing your goals, if you find that that you are not able to complete a particular step along the path to your goal, take a closer look at it. It is possible that the step was too big, so do not be afraid to break it down further and go from there. It could also be that the step was not SMART from the start. See if you can rework it to make it one you can tackle.

Learning goal setting skills takes practice, but can be

invaluable in helping you do those things you have been avoiding or "just don't seem to get to" and feel a sense of accomplishment. Consider consulting with a CBT therapist if you think therapy may be helpful for you in reaching your goals.

Understanding the importance of Goal setting

A lot a people who come for therapy it is usually because their relationships are suffering, and so they are suffering. It could be a teenaged boy whose severe social anxiety prevents him from spending time with his friends, a woman with depression that makes it hard to be the partner she wants to be, a father whose expressions of anger have put distance between him and his kids, or the college student whose alcohol-fueled behavior has alienated her friends. It's hard for our relationships to thrive when we're hurting.

Effective therapy can improve our relationships, whether or not those relationships are the specific target of the treatment. A relatively brief course of cognitive behavioral therapy (CBT)—which has been tested more than any other treatment—can lead to marked benefits not only for the person in therapy but for those close to that person. Some of the major relationship benefits of CBT include:

1. Greater presence. It's hard to overstate the importance of our presence in a relationship, since we can't truly "relate" to someone who's not there. One of

the biggest complaints about partners that I hear in my practice is that "s/he isn't there for me". Sometimes the person means quite literally that their partner is absent—always traveling for work, for example. Just as often the problem is that even when the person is there in body, his or her mind is elsewhere.

Mindfulness-based CBT can address both of these issues; for example, training in mindfulness has been shown in multiple studies to increase one's ability to attend to the person we're with. A CBT framework can help translate one's intention to be present into a plan of action to make it happen.

Try it: The next time your partner talks with you about something, bring your full attention to what they're saying. Practice seeing the person as though for the first time, really focusing on them and what they're saying.

2. Less anxiety. When we're overwhelmed by anxiety, we're not our best selves. It's no surprise that untreated anxiety disorders take a toll on our closest relationships. For example, the need for a "safety companion" in panic disorder and agoraphobia can lead to strain as the supporting partner has to adjust his or her schedule to accommodate the other person's travels. Similarly the chronic worry in generalized anxiety disorder frequently leads to tension and irritability, causing conflict between partners.

For any anxiety diagnosis, the treatments with the most evidence for their effectiveness come from CBT. The relief a person feels from a marked reduction in anxiety extends to greater harmony in the relationship.

Try it: If you've struggled with uncontrollable anxiety, consider looking into the best treatments for your condition on the website for Division 12 of the American Psychological Association. You can also search the therapist directory of PsychologyToday.com for a therapist who provides the treatment you're looking for. If a suitable therapist is not available, you might pursue self-guided CBT (such as with this book), which has been shown to be effective.

3. Improved mood. As with anxiety, untreated depression wears on couples. It's a struggle to be the partner we're capable of being when we have no energy, little enthusiasm even for activities we would normally enjoy, and no sex drive, among other symptoms. After a typical course of CBT for depression—12 to 16 weeks—the average person will not only feel substantially better but will be able to function much more effectively and happier individuals make happier couples.

Try it: As with anxiety, you can search for a CBT therapist through the PsychologyToday.com therapist directory. There is also evidence that self-guided CBT can be effective for treating depression (e.g., CBT in 7 Weeks or Cognitive Behavioural Therapy), so CBT is available even when a therapist is not. You can even do Internet-based CBT (Be always careful for the Internet-based information)

4. Better sleep. As many as 23% of adults in the US suffered from bad sleep in the past month. When we're not sleeping well we tend to be cranky and impatient—not a recipe for the best interactions with the people who love us. Furthermore, insomnia can turn the bed into a place of worry and stress, which interferes with a cozy night's sleep beside our partner. CBT for insomnia (CBT-I) is typically 4 to 6 sessions and is the treatment of choice for insomnia. It helps a person fall asleep faster and sleep more soundly, and restores a strong association between the bed and sleep. And better sleep helps with pretty much everything.

Try it: If you've struggled with sleep, consult these guidelines for healthy sleep habits. The National Sleep Foundation has suggestions for finding a CBT-I therapist. CBT-I is also available through self-guided books (e.g., End the Insomnia Struggle) and apps.

5. Healthier relationship with alcohol. Problematic drinking can kill a relationship. Alcohol use disorder is tied to higher divorce rates, greater intimate partner violence, lower relationship satisfaction, and a host of

other problems. CBT can effectively target the thoughts and behaviors that maintain problems with alcohol, and replace drinking with healthier ways of coping. Interestingly, the treatment with the strongest research evidence is Behavioral Couples Therapy, with both the patient and his or her partner actively involved in the treatment.

For many individuals with an alcohol use disorder, lifelong abstinence is necessary. However, there is modest support for a treatment program that includes the possibility of moderate alcohol consumption for some people.

Try it: If you're interested in learning more about the Moderate Drinking program, some information are in this book (but not all the necessary ones so look for something more specific). You can also consult the PsychologyToday.com directory to find a therapist who provides Behavioral Couples Therapy for alcohol use disorders.

6. Happier kids. When a child is struggling with intense fears (e.g., phobias, obsessive-compulsive disorder), it can lead to tremendous stress for the family. Parents inevitably feel the strain when a child is refusing to go to school, struggling socially, or having problems at bedtime. As the saying goes, "You're only as happy as your least happy child."

Furthermore, most couples have somewhat different parenting styles, with one partner more lenient and the other more of the disciplinarian. A child's intense struggles will tend to amplify these differences, leading to conflict between the parents. At the end of the night when the kids are finally in bed and both parents just want to unwind, they may instead find themselves arguing about how best to help their child. Thus they may feel like their reserves are exhausted, with little left to give their child or each other.

The American Academy of Child and Adolescent Psychiatry recommends CBT as a first-line approach for treating many childhood conditions, including anxiety and OCD. Similarly, the American Academy of Sleep Medicine recommends behavioral treatments for sleep problems in infants and children, which can help both the child and the parents sleep through the night.

Try it: There are books available that detail how to apply the techniques of CBT to help your child with anxiety (e.g., Helping Your Anxious Child) or OCD (e.g., What to Do When Your Brain Gets Stuck). There are also many CBT-focused web resources available, such as from the International OCD Foundation and the Society of Clinical Child and Adolescent Psychology.

7. Healthier Thought Patterns. Even if we're not dealing with a diagnosable condition like anxiety, depression, insomnia, or a substance use disorder, the tools of CBT can have powerful effects on our

relationships. CBT is based on an understanding of the connections among thoughts, feelings, and behaviors. When our thought patterns are aligned with reality, they generally lead to positive feelings and behaviors. However, when our thoughts become distorted in some way, they start to work against us, including in our relationships.

For example, we might notice that our partner left his clothes on the floor and think, "He expects me to pick up after him. He thinks I'm his maid." The result might include a fight driven by resentment and defensiveness. Or we could think that our partner seems distant and tell ourselves, "She's unhappy with me and our relationship," leading us to withdraw in turn.

The cognitive part of CBT encourages us first of all to notice the thoughts we're telling ourselves; oftentimes they happen so quickly and automatically that we don't even recognize the story our mind is creating. Once we've identified the thoughts we can test them out to see if they're accurate. Maybe our partner's clothes on the floor say nothing about his view of us, or expectations that we clean up his mess. And perhaps our partner's preoccupation has nothing to do with our relationship and everything to do with her worries about her ailing mother. With practice we can replace distorted and destructive thoughts with more accurate and constructive ones.

(Importantly, cognitive techniques are not about fooling ourselves or pretending things are better than they are. It would be important to know if our thoughts are actually valid so we can deal with the situation directly.)

Try it: The next time you're upset with your partner, write down the thoughts you notice and the emotions you feel. Then ask yourself the following questions (adapted from Retrain Your Brain: Cognitive Behavioral Therapy in 7 Weeks):

What is the evidence for my thought?

Is there evidence that contradicts my thought?

Based on the evidence, how accurate is the thought?

How could I modify this thought to make it fit better with reality?

8. Greater enactment of our intentions. All of us want to be the best significant other we can be. We want to be attentive, supportive, generous, patient. And like anything else, the road to impoverished relationships is paved with the best of intentions. If we're not deliberate about living out our values, we risk leaving them in the abstract—vague platitudes without substance.

For example, we might tell ourselves, "My family matters to me more than anything," and then live as though family is our last priority. We might idealize presence in our relationship yet attend more to our phone than to those around us.

The tools of CBT can help even when there is no "disorder"—when we simply want to commit to sustained action that supports our deepest values. It starts with taking an inventory of our relationship, and setting clearly defined goals based on what we find— for example, To listen when my spouse talks to me. It includes identifying specific behaviors we want to practice that will move us toward our goals.

We might plan, for instance, to turn off our phone during dinner and focus on our conversation. The goals and activities can be anything that's important to us in our relationship—we get to decide. It can be very beneficial to collaborate with our partner in the process by asking what they need more of from us.

A CBT approach also includes planning activities as specifically as possible so they stay on our radar, like putting "Come home early to make dinner" in our calendar, and protecting the time. Through daily practice of our intentions, we give our relationship the nourishment it needs not only to last but to be extraordinary.

CHAPTER FOUR

CBT FAQS

Answers to frequently asked questions about CBT, such as how to find a therapist and what to expect in treatment, are outlined below.

How will I know if CBT is for me?

Although many people can benefit from CBT, not everyone finds it helpful. You might find that it just doesn't suit you, or doesn't meet your needs.

I think it can go either way. I've been through a long course of CBT a few years ago, and for some people it helped, whereas for others it didn't.

Before deciding to have CBT, it might be helpful to think about the following:

Is short-term therapy right for me? If you have severe or complex problems, you may find a short-term therapy like CBT is less helpful. Sometimes, therapy may need to go on for longer to cover fully the number of problems you have, and the length of time they've been around.

Am I comfortable thinking about my feelings? CBT can involve becoming aware of your anxieties and emotions. Initially, you may find this process uncomfortable or distressing.

How much time do I want to spend? CBT can involve exercises for you to do outside of your sessions with a therapist. You may find this means you need to commit your own time to complete the work over the course of treatment, and afterwards.

Do I have a clear problem to solve? You may find CBT is less suitable if you feel generally unhappy or unfulfilled, but don't have troubling symptoms or a particular aspect of your life you want to work on.

Most people know within the first few sessions if they are comfortable with CBT and whether it is meeting their treatment needs. The therapist will also check to see that CBT is the right "fit" for you. When the fit is not quite right, the therapist may adjust the treatment or suggest other treatment options. However, in general, CBT may be a good therapy option for you if:

You are interested in learning practical skills to manage your present, day-to-day life and associated emotional difficulties.

You are willing and interested in practising change strategies ("homework") between sessions to consolidate improvement.

CBT may not be for you if you want to focus exclusively on past issues, if you want supportive counselling, or if you are not willing to do homework between sessions.

How can I find a qualified CBT therapist in my area?

It is most probably wise when seeking a therapist who provides CBT to try and assess which of the above-mentioned categories they may fall into. Many therapists will report that they use CBT, but few have actually had specific supervised training in the model and many do not provide cutting-edge treatments for specific disorders.

In addition, it would also be important to check whether or not the therapist has specific experience in your area of concern. For instance, an individual may have plenty of experience in working with anxiety or depression, but little experience or expertise in treating tic disorders, insomnia or psychosis, for example. Below is a list of reasonable questions that one could ask a therapist prior to making an appointment or during an initial appointment aimed at assessing their experience with CBT.

Have you received any training in CBT?

Training could vary from an introduction during a masters programme to an internationally-certified qualification.

Did your training include individual supervision of case material from an experienced or internationally-certified CBT therapist?

It is important to distinguish between theoretical training and practical, supervised training that includes individual supervision in the use of CBT in working with clients.

Does your CBT training include international certification from an international training standards committee?

Typical international certification is from the Beck Institute or the Albert Ellis Institute. Other training centres in the USA and the UK also exist.

How many years' experience do you have in practising CBT?

We all start with little experience and build our knowledge base. It would be wise not to doubt a well-trained and supervised CBT therapist with one or two years' experience. It, however, goes without saying that those therapists with greater practical experience bring the expertise accumulated from this experience to helping you.

In what way do you use CBT in your practice?

Many people will tell you that they integrate CBT in to their practice. This typically would entail using skills or techniques from more than one theoretical orientation at the same time. This approach is known as eclecticism. This is not unethical nor an unacceptable practice. Should you look for a CBT therapist specifically, this is obviously not the type of service provided by a therapist with an eclectic approach. Therapists will also tell you that they use different theoretical approaches to treat different clients and problems. This is also an acceptable approach. It would, however, be important to determine if the therapist is sufficiently trained in CBT and if the therapist would suggest CBT for your specific problem.

Ask if the therapist has training in the CBT treatment of your specific disorder.

It important to know that the therapist has disorder-specific training in the condition that you require help with.

To find the contact information for certified CBT therapists in Canada and the United States, consult the following resources:

Academy of Cognitive Therapies
www.academyofct.org

Association for Behaviour and Cognitive Therapies
www.abct.org

What can I expect on my first visit with a CBT therapist?

You will meet your therapist and they will introduce themselves, ask for your preferred name and help you to feel at ease. They may also introduce a little bit about what CBT is and the way that the sessions will be. You do not need to know anything about CBT before you begin your therapy and your therapist should explain it in an easy-to-understand way.

Your therapist will talk to you about confidentiality, the number of sessions you may work towards, how often your sessions will be, how long they will last, how to cancel appointments and what happens if you miss an appointment.

Your therapist will usually have the information you gave at your initial screening appointment but may ask you a little more about the main problem you would like some help with and about you and your circumstances. This is not to get you to 'tell your story all over again', but to help you and your therapist reach an understanding of how you will work together and what you will focus on within the sessions.

Your therapist may also ask you to think of some positive goals so that you have something you are working towards. This can help you to connect with something important to you or to work towards something you would like to do if you no longer had the problem.

Your therapist may talk to you about 'homework'. Homework is an integral part of CBT and after each session you will think with your therapist about how you can apply the things you have done in the session to your day-to-day life. After your first appointment, you may be asked to keep a monitoring diary or to read some information/handouts relevant to your problem.

You will do the same questionnaires you completed at your first appointment. These will be asked at every appointment to help you and your therapist keep track of your progress. You may sometimes be asked to do an additional questionnaire more specific to your problem, however, this will vary from client to client.

Your therapist will check with you if you are at any risk to yourself or from anyone else. This is something we ask every client so that we can help you to stay safe.

You will make your next appointment with your therapist.

Your therapist will go at a pace that suits you and the above points are a guide only. You may do more or less than this in your first appointment and that is OK. You can also ask questions and express any concerns about therapy at any time in your appointment. Your therapist wants to work with you as a together to help with your recovery. While your therapist can offer ideas about what has helped others with similar problems in the past, they also know that you are the expert in your problem and how it affects you, and you should both be playing an active role in therapy together.

What happens in a CBT session?

CBT sessions can be given to clients individually or in groups. Both formats follow the same predictable structure, as follows:

Mood check: The therapist asks about your mood since the previous session. This may include the use of scales to assess depression, anxiety or other emotional problems. The purpose of the mood check is to see if your mood improves from session to session.

Bridge: The focus of the previous session is reviewed to create a bridge to the current session.

Agenda: The therapist and client identify issues to address in the current session that will act as the agenda.

Homework review: Homework from the previous session is reviewed to note progress and troubleshoot any difficulties that may have emerged.

Agenda items: Agenda issues are addressed using cognitive and behavioural strategies.

New homework: Exercises and tasks for the upcoming week are assigned.

Summary and client feedback: Wrap up of the session.

How can I get the most out of CBT between sessions?

CBT is a treatment approach that teaches you skills to become your own therapist over time. You learn new skills in the therapy sessions, but ultimately much of the change occurs between therapy sessions when practising the skills in your own environment as part of homework. Early in treatment, the CBT therapist will suggest homework, such as monitoring thoughts and behaviours, taking steps to reduce avoidance behaviour, conducting experiments to test out predictions and completing worksheets to challenge negative thoughts or beliefs. As treatment progresses, you will learn to set your own homework between sessions to help you accomplish your treatment goals. Research demonstrates that the more you successfully practise the skills of CBT in your homework, the better the treatment outcome.

How frequent are the sessions?

CBT usually starts out with weekly sessions. As treatment progresses, sessions may be spaced further apart, such as every two weeks or month. Once people have finished a course of CBT, it is common for them to return for occasional "booster" sessions to keep up their progress, deal with any setbacks and prevent relapse of problems. Again, hospital-based programs are typically pre-set (e.g., a group meeting weekly at the same time for 12 weeks) and are less flexible in terms of scheduling and spacing sessions than community-based CBT therapists.

Do I need to prepare for CBT sessions?

Preparing to discuss a specific problem at each session helps you to get the most out of CBT. Coming prepared helps to keep you focused on your goals for therapy. It also helps to build a therapeutic relationship between you and your therapist and to communicate well throughout the session.

Will the CBT therapist be able to understand and appreciate my own unique background?

Research on CBT demonstrates that it is an effective treatment regardless of gender, race, ethnicity, culture, sexual orientation or social economic status. CBT therapists are trained to recognize the importance of cultural values and to adapt their treatments to meet culturally unique needs. They are trained, for example, to:

Be aware of their own personal values and biases and how these may influence their relationship with the client.

Use skills and intervention strategies that are culturally appropriate for the person being seen.

Be aware of how certain cultural processes may influence the relationship between the therapist and client.

As a client in CBT you should feel that you can openly discuss aspects of your culture or sexual orientation, for example, and that your treatment will be delivered in a manner that is consistent with these values.

Is CBT an effective treatment for children and adolescents?

CBT has been adapted for use with children and has been shown in research to be an effective intervention for a variety of clinical problems that can emerge in childhood, including anxiety and depression. The content and pacing of the therapy is adjusted to be appropriate for the child's level of development. Often, the CBT therapist will work with the parent and child—the younger the child, the more involved the parent will be in learning and delivering CBT strategies for their child's problem.

What are the common barriers that come up in CBT?

Barriers to treatment can include:

- Perceived stigma associated with mental health treatment

- Difficulty identifying and distinguishing emotions and their intensity

- Difficulty in reflecting on thoughts

- Difficulty tolerating heightened emotions

- Not completing homework

- Financial constraints

- Chronic conditions and multiple difficulties

- Low optimism toward improving

- Avoiding treatment sessions.

The therapist will work with you to reduce these barriers and will also offer strategies that you can use to overcome barriers.

Should I start treatment with medications or CBT or both in combination?

Many people who seek treatment for emotional difficulties in Canada are first treated by their family doctor with one or more medications (e.g., antidepressants) before CBT is considered. Not much research has been done to show whether it is best to start treatment with medication or CBT or both. However, research has shown that CBT, with or without certain types of medications, is equally effective for the treatment of anxiety problems, and that CBT and medications together are best for treating severe depression and psychosis. Importantly, taking these kinds of medications has not been shown to interfere with CBT, and in some instances may help people to get more out of the therapy.

There is, however, one class of medication commonly prescribed to people with anxiety problems, known as benzodiazepines, which can potentially limit the benefits of CBT. Medications in this class include clonazepam (Rivotril), alprazolam (Xanax) and lorazepam (Ativan). While these medications can rapidly relieve and control anxiety in the short term, they can also make it harder to learn new things, which is essential to benefit from CBT and reduce anxiety in the long run. If you are taking these medications and are about to start CBT, your CBT therapist will want to review the advantages and disadvantages of continuing with these medications during CBT treatment.

When considering or starting CBT, discuss all of your questions or concerns about your medications with your CBT therapist and/ or your prescribing medical doctor. Medications can be monitored and discussed throughout treatment and adjusted depending on your progress in CBT. Note that recommendations or changes to your medication can only be made by your prescribing doctor. If your CBT therapist is not a doctor, he or she can—with your permission— communicate with your doctor to help ensure that you receive the optimal combination of treatments.

How can I stay well after finishing CBT?

A major goal of CBT is for you to become your own therapist and to continue to practise CBT skills even after you are feeling better. You may also wish to return for follow-up or "booster" sessions from time to time. A key component of CBT treatment is teaching relapse prevention strategies. This includes helping you learn to identify the triggers and early signs of relapse and to develop an action plan to prevent downward spirals of negative emotions.

CHAPTER FIVE

ALTERNATIVE COGNITIVE BEHAVIOURAL APPROACHES

Of the hundreds of psychological treatments available, several are closely related to CBT, but have distinct approaches. Although the effectiveness of these alternative CBT approaches is not as well proven as the mainstream approach described so far in this guide, the four introduced on the following pages have been found to be effective in helping people with certain types of problems. Overall, they all share a common goal of helping people learn how to "let go" of focusing on and reacting to their thoughts.

Mindfulness therapy and mindfulness based cognitive therapy

Mindfulness techniques can be used to help people distance themselves from their negative thinking and recognize that thoughts do not have to determine behaviours. Mindfulness is a state of awareness, openness and receptiveness that allows people to engage fully in what they are doing at any given moment. Mindfulness skills are mainly taught through meditation; however, other experiential exercises (e.g., walking or eating with awareness) can also be used to teach these skills.

A middle aged woman is feeling overwhelmed, anxious, depressed, hopeless and depleted of all of her energy. She explains to her doctor that she has been having feelings of self doubt and is desperate to turn back the clock to a time in her twenties and thirties when she knew she was "beautiful", "thin", and "revered". She has tried everything from Pilates, energy healing, life coaching, herbal remedies, hypnotherapy, Reiki, and has visited an array of holistic spas and retreats.

Yet she continues to fee chronic emptiness and impending doom. It is as if she is suffering from a should sickness. Not doubt the alternative treatments were effective, at least initially. But the days of long-lost youth and feelings of worthlessness returned. When her psychotherapist recommends learning mindfulness meditations, she agrees in her desperation.

Psychotherapy and pharmacological solutions are some of the common treatment options for patients with mental disorders. But, alternative treatments for psychiatric conditions are increasingly becoming popular. Lately, doctors have been advising alternative treatments, like meditation and yoga, for mental issues, particularly for anxiety disorders and depression.

According to a recent study published in the Journal of Child and Adolescent Psychopharmacology, significant changes were evident in the brain regions that control emotional processing of youths who were given mindfulness-based therapies.

Though anxiety disorders are common among children and adolescents, antidepressants administered to treat the condition are many a times not tolerated well by children who are at a high risk of developing bipolar disorder.

So, the researchers at the University of Cincinnati (UC) have now found out how cognitive therapy that utilizes mindfulness techniques, such as meditation, quiet reflection, and facilitator-led discussion, may help as an adjunct to pharmacological interventions. The study was part of a larger investigation to understand the effectiveness of mindfulness-based therapy.

The respondents were chosen from a group of youths who had anxiety disorders (generalized, social and/or separation anxiety) and who have a parent with bipolar disorder. The study, published in the Journal of Child and Adolescent Psychopharmacology in July 2016, tried to evaluate neurophysiology of mindfulness-based cognitive therapy in children who had higher risks of developing bipolar disorder.

Mindfulness therapy increases activity in brain

The nine participants aged 9-16 years were made to undergo functional magnetic resonance imaging (fMRI) while they were involved in a continuous performance of tasks with emotional and neutral distractors prior to and following 12 weeks of mindfulness-based cognitive therapy.

"Our preliminary observation that the mindfulness therapy increases activity in the part of the brain known as the cingulate, which processes cognitive and emotional information, is noteworthy," said co-principal researcher of the study Jeffrey Strawn, M.D., an associate professor in the Department of Psychiatry and Behavioral Neuroscience, and director of the Anxiety Disorders Research Program.

"This study, taken together with previous research, raises the possibility that treatment-related increases in brain activity (of the anterior cingulate cortex) during emotional processing may improve emotional processing in anxious youth who are at risk for developing bipolar disorder," he added.

Speaking about the effectiveness of mindfulness techniques, co-author of the study Sian Cotton, Ph.D., an associate professor of family and community medicine at UC, said, "Mindfulness-based therapeutic interventions promote the use of meditative practices to increase present-moment awareness of conscious thoughts, feelings and body sensations in an effort to manage negative experiences more effectively." These alternative approaches augment traditional treatments offering new strategies for coping with psychological problems, he said.

Recovery roadmap

The researchers noted that increases in mindfulness were associated with decreases in anxiety in the participants.

However, the researchers called for further studies into this for more clarity. "The path from an initial understanding of the effects of psychotherapy on brain activity to the identification of markers of treatment response is a challenging one, and will require additional studies of specific aspects of emotional processing circuits," Strawn said.

For any mental health condition, be it anxiety disorder or depression, early intervention is the key. Hence, if a loved one is exhibiting any psychiatric symptom, seek the advice of a doctor immediately.

Mindfulness skills can be broken down into three categories:

Defusion: distancing oneself from and letting go of unhelpful thoughts, beliefs and memories.

Acceptance: accepting thoughts and feelings without judgment, simply allowing them to come and go rather than trying to push them out of awareness or make sense of them.

Contact in the present moment: engaging fully in the here-and-now with an attitude of openness and curiosity.

Mindfulness skills promote freedom from the tendency to get drawn into automatic negative reactions to thoughts and feelings.

Mindfulness techniques have been used in the treatment of chronic pain, hypertension, heart disease, cancer, gastrointestinal disorders, eating disorders, anxiety disorders and substance use disorders. Mindfulness-based cognitive therapy has been found to be effective in reducing relapse to depression.

Acceptance and commitment therapy

While some therapies attempt to change upsetting thoughts and feelings, acceptance and commitment therapy (act) helps people to simply notice and accept thoughts and feelings in the present moment.

ACT views psychological suffering as being caused by avoiding or evaluating thoughts and feelings, which in turn can lead to ways of thinking that interfere with our ability to act consistently with important personal values. The focus of act is on helping people accept what is out of their personal control while committing to doing what is within their control to improve their quality of life.

ACT aims to help people handle the pain and stress that life inevitably brings and to create a rich, full and meaningful life. People learn how to deal with painful thoughts and feelings in ways that have less impact and influence over their lives. For example, they learn to:

- Distance themselves from upsetting thoughts (cognitive defusion)

- Accept experiences in the present moment

- Discover important and meaningful personal values

- Set goals consistent with these values

- Commit to take action

ACT has been found to be effective in treating depression, anxiety, stress, chronic pain and substance use disorders.

Dialectical behavioural therapy

Dialectical behavioural therapy (dbt) is an effective treatment for people with excessive mood swings, self-harming behaviour and other interpersonal problems related to the expression of anger.

DBT has an individual and a group component. In individual therapy, the therapist and client follow a treatment target hierarchy to guide their discussion of issues that come up between weekly sessions. First priority is given to self-harming and suicidal behaviours, then to behaviours that interfere with therapy, and next to improving the client's quality of life. The quality-of-life improvement part of the therapy involves identifying skills that the person has but is not using to full advantage, to teaching new skills, and to discussing obstacles for using those skills. Weekly group therapy focuses on acquiring new skills.

Clients keep diary cards to help monitor their use of the skills and have access to 24-hour phone consultation with their therapist.

The four modules of dbt are core mindfulness, emotion regulation (e.g., identifying and labelling emotions and reducing vulnerability to negative emotions), interpersonal effectiveness (e.g., assertiveness skills) and distress tolerance skills (e.g., crisis survival skills such as distracting, self-soothing and improving the moment).

Meta-cognitive therapy

Metacognitive therapy is sometimes described as a type of therapy that involves changing how people think rather than what they are thinking about. In this way, metacognitive therapy is distinct from cognitive behavioral therapy, which focuses more on the content of people's thoughts.

Two psychologists, Dr. Adrian Wells of the University of Manchester and Dr. Gerald Matthews of the University of Cincinnati, developed the theory underlying metacognitive therapy in the early 1990s. Initially intended only for patients with generalized anxiety disorder, metacognitive therapy has since been adapted for use in treating a variety of mental health problems.

According to metacognitive theory, maladaptive thinking that occurs in various psychiatric disorders tends to take on a life of its own, growing from thoughts about a specific situation to a more global world view. For example, people who are anxious may initially worry about external situations, such as missing a train. With time, however, they may begin to develop a second type of worry, focused on their own thought processes. In essence, according to this theory, they begin to worry about being worried.

In people with attention deficit hyperactivity disorder (ADHD), problems with metacognition more often encompass difficulty in planning or executing tasks. The goal of metacognitive therapy in ADHD is to improve organization skills, planning, and time management.

Most of the research evaluating metacognitive therapy has focused on anxiety disorders such as social phobia, post-traumatic stress disorder, and generalized anxiety disorder. Only a few studies have evaluated its use in helping adults with ADHD (none have been conducted in children). The research is therefore preliminary, but so far promising.

In one study, researchers at the Mount Sinai School of Medicine recruited 88 adult participants with ADHD, diagnosed using a structured interview based on criteria in the Diagnostic and Statistical Manual of Mental Disorders, Fourth Edition (DSM-IV). The group was carefully selected; few had substance abuse or other types of coexisting psychiatric disorders, which is more the norm in the community. The researchers randomly assigned half of the participants to metacognitive therapy and the others to supportive therapy, both offered in group formats consisting of 12 weekly sessions.

Those assigned to metacognitive therapy underwent a sequence of sessions designed to begin with learning specific skill sets (such as using a daily planner) and then progressing to broader abilities (organizing and executing a complex project). Those assigned to supportive therapy received encouragement and reinforcement of productive behaviors.

Some participants improved after both interventions, but those assigned to metacognitive therapy showed a greater degree of improvement on both objectively rated and self-perceived measures of organization, ability to complete tasks, and other practical components of attention skill. A greater proportion of people assigned to metacognitive therapy responded to therapy, defined as at least a 30% improvement in ADHD symptoms. In all, 19 of 41 (42%) of participants who completed metacognitive therapy responded, compared with five of 40 (12%) of those who completed supportive therapy.

This suggests that metacognitive therapy may indeed help some adult patients with ADHD. But before your husband tries it, just be aware that there are no long-term data about whether the potential benefits are retained over time. Your husband may also find it helpful to investigate other options to improve organization skills, such as cognitive behavioral therapy or coaching.

Meta-cognitive therapy (mct) was first developed to treat generalized anxiety disorder and is now also used to treat other anxiety disorders and depression.

Metacognition is the aspect of cognition that controls mental processes and thinking. Most people have some direct conscious experience of metacognition. For example, when a name is on the "tip of your tongue," metacognition is working to inform you that the information is somewhere in memory, even though you are unable to remember it.

People with depression or anxiety often feel as though they have lost control over their thoughts and behaviours. Their thinking and attention become fixed in patterns of brooding and dwelling on themselves and on threatening information. They develop coping behaviours that they believe are helpful, but that can actually worsen and prolong emotional distress. This pattern of thinking is called cognitive-attentional syndrome (cas).

In mct, people learn to reduce the cas by developing new ways of controlling their thinking and attention and of relating to depressive or anxious thoughts and beliefs. They also learn to modify the beliefs that give rise to the cas.

CHAPTER 6

APPLYING COGNITIVE BEHAVIORAL THERAPY (CBT) TO OVER-THINK NEGATIVE PATTERNS

Negative thinking can slow down the recovery of depression, and the reason is clear: If you think negative thoughts, you are more likely to remain depressed. But the way people with depression deal with positive emotions is less obvious. Researchers made a surprising observation: People with depression don't lack positive emotions, they just can't feel them. This cognitive style is called "dampening," it involves suppressing positive emotions with thoughts such as "I don't deserve to be happy" or "This good feeling won't last." For example, a new mother with postpartum depression may say she doesn't deserve to recover because she's a bad mother because she's depressed. Why do depressed people think so? We refers to this negative voice as a defensive pessimism-protection against high hopes. "you don't want to be foolish, so you use positive thoughts to protect yourself from possible disappointment."

How CBT can help with negative depression

Depression therapy has been found to be significantly helpful in treating depression. In CBT, you work together with your therapist to agree on behavior patterns that need to be changed. The objective is to recalibrate the part of your brain that holds happy thoughts so tightly.

"The root of the dampening effect could be an unexpected reaction to a major life event" through CBT, you and your therapist address it and work to put it into perspective." Regular CBT sessions and work you do on your own outside of therapy can help strengthen the new patterns: "It can be very liberating to be able to recognize these negative thoughts and leave them behind,"

CBT Techniques to Counteract the Negative Thinking of Depression

It was discovered that people with depression rarely respond well to self-study by CBT techniques to counteract negative thinking about depression. For this reason, we recommend that at least six weeks be committed to CBT. Your therapist will teach you CBT strategies to counteract depression-related negative thinking. She or he can also help you keep track of the techniques. You may end up working on five CBT strategies with your therapist:

Locate the problem and brainstorm solutions.

Journaling with your therapist and talking can help you discover the root of your depression. Once you have an idea, write down exactly what disturbs you in a simple phrase and think about ways to improve the problem. A hallmark of depression is despair-an unbelief that things can ever get better. Writing a list of things you can do to improve a situation can help ease the feelings of depression. If you are fighting for loneliness, for example, action steps to try may include joining a local club based on your interests or signing up for online dating. Write self-declarations to counter negative thoughts. After finding your depression's root problems, think about the negative thoughts you use to dampen positive thoughts.

Write a self-declaration to counteract any negative thinking.

Remember your self-statements and repeat them to yourself when you see the little voice creeping in your head to snuff out a positive thought. You will create new associations in time to replace negative thoughts with positive ones.

The self-declaration should not be too far from negative thinking, or the mind may not accept it. For example, if the negative thought is, "I'm so depressed right now," instead of saying, "I'm really happy now," it could be better to say, "Every life has ups and downs, and mine also has ups and downs." At the same time, your mind applauds the fact that joy is kept in check to protect against disappointment. "Recognizing that part of you is trying to do something healthy is okay."

Self-reporting is sometimes too routine and needs to be refreshed. We recommend that you translate your self-declarations into other languages you can speak or rephrase, possibly even bumping up your joyful feelings. "For example, the self-statement" it's okay to explore my ups" may turn out to be "it's okay to have a super "up" day."

Find new opportunities to think positive thoughts.

People who enter a room and immediately think, "I hate the color of the wall," could instead train to locate five things in the room they feel positive as quickly as possible. Set your phone to remind you of something positive three times a day. It recommends that someone else work on the same technique should "buddy up." You and your friend can be excited to share positive thoughts and experiences throughout the day.

Complete every day by visualizing the best parts.

At the end of each day, write down the things you're most grateful for in your life or type them into an online journal. The recording of positive thoughts and even sharing them online can help you form new associations in your mind or create new paths. Someone who created a new way of thinking could wake up in the morning and think, "Ugh, another working day "to "What a beautiful day it is."

Learn to accept disappointment as a normal part of life.

Deceptive situations are part of life and your response can affect how fast you can move forward. Someone who goes through a breakup may blame him or herself or even gain weight, saying, "What's the point of looking good? I'll never meet anyone else. "Maybe a better approach is to be disappointed and remember that some things are out of your control. Work on what is in your control: Write down what happened, what you learned from the experience and what you can do next time differently, taking care of overly negative thoughts. This can help you to move forward and feel better about your future.

Cognitive behavioral therapy Effective tips

Research has shown that we can have better control of thoughts and feelings by identifying our distorted thoughts and beliefs. Having distorted thoughts or beliefs doesn't mean we're wrong. At different times in our lives, we have all distorted thoughts and beliefs. Examples of distorted thoughts:

Over-generalization

Sometimes we can see things as everything or nothing. If one thing goes wrong with a project, for example, we may think the whole project is a failure.

Or, if there's one thing that upsets us about a person, we can decide that we don't care about him.

Mind Reading

We assume we know what someone thinks. We can say that someone thinks we're "stupid "or doesn't like us, even if there's no evidence to support this thought. That's called reading the mind. We exaggerate how "abhorrent "something is or imagine the worst outcome possible. Maybe our boss wants to talk to us and we're disastrous to be fired. Or, it's raining on one of the holidays and we think "this is the worst thing that could have happened."

Fortune Telling

We think we surely know what will happen. We say, for example, "I know I won't get this promotion "or "I won't be able to handle this task." Specific behaviors or skills, including social skills, assertiveness, organizational skills and relaxation techniques, are also taught. During and between sessions, these are taught. Below, there are seven pearls I will share with you that I have found useful in my practice over the years:

Discuss treatment goals

During the initial evaluation phase, it is important to work together on treatment goals. This helps to maintain focused and productive treatment. Therapy can end up focusing on any problem that arises this week without objectives and can interfere with the progress of the original problems presented. Sometimes the patient may not be able to describe a goal specifically except for a vague "I want to be less anxious "or "I want to be happier." It's okay at the start. However, you should return to this discussion about goals in the first couple of months to see if they can be described in more specific terms. For example, if someone has depression, the goals may include: Finding a fuller job, going back to college, exercising three times a week, making two new friends and stopping marijuana use.

Each session with an agenda

Each session should begin with a collaborative agenda between the therapist and the patient. Again, this helps to focus and make the session more efficient. The agenda should include follow-up on previous session homework, check-in on mood and week, bridging or reviewing the topics and progress from the previous session, and topics related to the current session, which are related to a specific objective.

Discuss where to address the issue

Most therapeutic objectives will have several components, including distorted thoughts, beliefs or behaviours. Therefore, during the session, decide collaboratively on which level to meet the objectives. If you work on distorted thoughts, it is important to determine which thoughts or images lead to distress, such as anxiety, low mood or a certain behavior. If you work on certain behaviors such as social skills or relationship problems, it is important to discuss when the skills are used and how likely they are used. Another useful technique for addressing behaviors is the play of roles and visualization that helps to practice skills and address any behavioral blocks or anxieties.

Use Flashcards

Flashcards can be used to remember the session's key points or a mantra that can help with certain thoughts or feelings. If I work with a patient who is struggling with depression, I will name the flashcard something like "Survival Kit "and it will include strategies to cope with depression, such as reaching a friend, leaving the house, reaching me or taking care of a small chore.

Stay focused

At the start of treatment, therapeutic objectives are discussed. The therapy session can sometimes go in a direction unrelated to any of the treatment goals. This is appropriate at certain times, but if this happens every session and for the whole duration, the progress of therapy may be limited. In CBT, structure is important, but flexibility is also important. This would be a time to work together to discuss whether to continue with the current diversion or issue being discussed or to return to what has been discussed in the agenda.

Assign homework

A collaborative discussion on homework or "action tasks "takes place between sessions towards the end of each session. If one of the problems is time management or the recording of thoughts and images that occur during stressful periods in a notebook to discuss and address at the following session, an action task may be to buy a calendar. Always ensure that the homework or action task is monitored at the next session, or it creates the impression that working on problems or objectives between sessions is not a crucial part of improving.

Ask for feedback

At the end of the session, ask what was going well during the session, what could have gone better and what are the main messages to take away. This helps build the alliance, improve sessions in the future and maximize progress.

Cognitive behavioral therapy is a highly effective form of therapy with or without medicines and an excellent way to practice psychiatry.

Cognitive behavioral therapy at home Tips that can help ease your anxieties

CBT is based on the idea that our thoughts, emotions and behaviors are interconnected and that one can change the other. This may sound trendy, but it is also effective and has been studied rigorously. CBT varies from anxiety to depression to schizophrenia to substance use disorders for all types of mental health problems.

The goal is to learn skills to address real-life problems outside the therapist's office, Lindgren says. The more you practice, the more a habit will become of CBT skills.

"If you're someone who has good intentions but needs someone to be accountable, I'd meet a therapist" but if you know you're a good self-taught person, it's reasonable to think about doing it on your own."

Here are her tips for practicing at home (or wherever you are).

Change your perspective

You can modify problem thoughts by using a technique called cognitive restructuring, which can help you change your behaviour. The next time you notice that you are anxious or depressed, ask yourself: What do I think about or what emotions do I struggle to make me feel like this? Notice if certain thoughts or memories cause distressing physical symptoms; you can even list them. This will help you understand how your emotions and thoughts are connected and what is triggering you.

Balance your thoughts

Many struggles in mental health involve thoughts or predictions that influence behavior that are distressing but inherently faulty. For example, if you're anxious when you're in crowds and actively avoid them, you might be told that if you tried to go to a crowded place-like a sports game or concert-you'd panic, do something to embarrass yourself, and you wouldn't enjoy it. This belief then strengthens your avoidance. Notice how your brain makes decisions based on fear or avoidance and then ask yourself: What is the evidence for this thought? Are there any cold, hard facts that things are going to go wrong, or do I just speculate? Consider if you could have other thoughts that would be more balanced or helpful. If you changed your thinking a little bit to be less frightening or negative, what new emotions could arise? If you work to balance your thoughts, your emotions and behaviors will probably follow.

Be patient with yourself

Change won't happen overnight, so don't expect it if you try CBT alone (or even with a therapist to guide you). Instead, your goal should be to develop your skills so that you feel better equipped to deal with any challenges your mental health wants to take. Focus on getting ready for small victories, then build up your goals slowly over time. Be proud of any positive change, however small it may seem. Recognize that progress is not linear; it will be easier for some weeks, harder for others, and that's normal.

Be kind to yourself

Without even realizing it, it's easy to get caught up in negative self-talk. But getting constantly on yourself won't inspire the confidence you need to make you feel better. When you notice negative thoughts-things like "Why can't I get it together?" or "other people have no problem "-replace them with something nicer. Ask yourself if your friends will ever tell you the things you say to yourself. No, no? So don't let yourself tell them either. This doesn't mean you should apologize for yourself if you made a mistake or did something wrong, but instead encourage you to cut the slack you usually reserve for others.

Do what you love

Anxiety, depression and other mental health struggles can remove the activities that matter to you in life, either because you are afraid of them or because you have no motivation to pursue them once. Maybe you liked reading, but now you're tired. Or you may have liked to go out with your friends, but now you're afraid to be away at night. Take the time to do one or two things regularly that always brought you joy and did your best to be present instead of being distracted or worried about the past. Then ask yourself how you feel you've done it. Did you feel better?

Be Self-aware

Maybe when you try to fall asleep or beat yourself over something you told a friend when you should finish an important work project, you're ruminating about work problems; either way, you're not focused on the moment. Instead, try switching your thoughts whenever they're not in line with what's going on right now. Ask yourself: Do my emotions reflect what's happening right now? If not, concentrate on the senses. What are you seeing and hearing? What's happening around you in the world? Instead of what happened in the past or what you're afraid will happen in the future, try to be aware of what's right before you.

A bright future

In the end, one of CBT's most powerful things is that it can give you hope.

"Inherently, it's optimistic. It teaches you to believe that change is possible and that you can change your life."

CHAPTER 7

MOST COMMON ERRORS MADE IN COGNITIVE-BEHAVIORAL THERAPY

In the course of my clinical practice, I have found a number of common errors that can prevent cognitive-behavioral therapy (CBT) from being as effective as it could be. The following describes these errors and how to correct them.

ERROR 1: Not Understanding the Necessity of Repetition for Change

A few years back when I was lecturing a group of psychiatric residents (future psychiatrists) about using CBT with sexually traumatized clients, one of the doctors stated "I tried that cognitive therapy with my patients and it doesn't work at all!" As I explored with her the specifics of what she had tried with her patients, I ascertained that, basically, she had told them how they should think and then expected them to change their thinking.

When I asked her what method she used to help them practice and repeat the new ways of thinking in daily life, she was speechless. I then explained that the key to successful cognitive therapy was repetition of the statements that challenge the irrational thinking and that the therapist must use a method to help clients do that.

People don't change their thinking just because they are told to think differently. If that was the case, most people wouldn't need CBT because someone else has probably already told them how they should think. The difference with CBT is that a variety of methods have been developed to provide the steps to change thinking.

The importance of repetition as a key component of CBT can't be emphasized enough. This is true of any new skill. When I was training for my black belt in Kenpo karate my instructor told me "When you have done this self-defense move 6,000 times, it will be automatic." And he was right! At first, I was awkward and slow in executing the movements. I had to think about every aspect of each move. I thought initially that it would never be automatic. However, I continued to practice. One day (after years of training) when I was teaching one of the brown belts, I realized that I was able to automatically respond to a wrist grab and put him on the ground without even thinking about it.

Changing your thinking is learning a new skill in the same way you learn a physical skill. You don't expect to be a proficient golfer without swinging the club a few thousand times. In fact, in the book "Outliers" by

Malcolm Gladwell, he sets the magic number for success at 10,000 hours. According to Gladwell, when we examine the lives of the most successful people in any sport or profession, we typically find that they have spent at least 10,000 hours honing their craft.

Certainly, that doesn't mean that it will take 10,000 hours to change your thinking and to have a positive impact on your life. In fact, with frequent repetition of the rational challenging thoughts you should notice changes in four to eight weeks. However, you will need more repetition than that for the new way of thinking to become automatic.

Think of it this way. How many hours have you spent in your lifetime repeating the detrimental irrational self-talk? You likely have become very automatic in that way of thinking so now you need to re-train your brain to think in a different way. To do that you need to identify specific thoughts that are beneficial and to deliberately think those thoughts repeatedly.

Sometimes it is difficult to achieve the necessary repetition especially when you are first learning. That is why reading articles about CBT or motivational thinking can be helpful. The more you read, the more repetition you obtain. Also, that is why I have created some audios that focus on changing thinking. The audios provide repetition without a great deal of effort.

ERROR 2: Making Assumptions about CBT Based on Social Comparision.

Many times when I first explain cognitive therapy to clients and we examine their irrational thinking and explain why it is irrational, they exclaim "That makes so much sense! I've never thought about it that way before!"

However, for some people, once they understand the process of using irrational thought challenges, they believe that that they should just be able to think that way without having to examine their thinking and deliberately change it. They make the mistake of using social comparison assumptions. In particular, they might state "I should be able to just think this way. Everyone else doesn't have to do this (referring to the CBT methods)."

What they don't realize is their assumptions about others not using CBT techniques is inaccurate. Just about anyone who is successful in life is using these techniques! However, they may not have been taught the techniques of CBT specifically and they may not know the terms such as "mind-reading" or "generalizing" but they are still using the methods.

I tend to think that CBT is just a compendium of methods that have helped people achieve success for thousands of years. For instance, if you read the "Tao te Ching" examining it for cognitive concepts, you will find that it contains all the same challenges to irrational thinking and methods of successful living that you will find in any book by Aaron Beck, Albert Ellis, or David Burns.

If you listen closely to people, you will begin to recognize how they apply these methods in their lives. For instance, I frequently hear people (outside of the office) say when describing a difficult event, "...but then I told myself..." In other words, they were using self-talk to cope with a situation. I've also heard people say things such as "Then I took a deep breath and..." describing how they calmed themselves before tackling a problem.

So don't assume that because you are having to learn these methods and deliberately apply them that you are doing something others don't have to do. The only difference is that you may not have learned the methods naturally while growing up and you are learning them now. You may not have had the role models or opportunities to learn these methods when you were young.

People aren't naturally successful. Anyone who is successful, whether in life, sports, career, or relationships, has learned these methods at some point in their lives and are applying them routinely.

ERROR 3: Not Making CBT Methods a Lifestyle Change

Many people don't realize that CBT is training the brain to react differently to situations. As a result, they often mistakenly believe that recognizing the error in thinking and correcting it a few times will impact a change in their life. After they have some initial benefit they may believe that it isn't necessary to continue practicing the methods.

However, cognitive-behavioral changes need to be thought of as lifestyle changes just as exercise or an effective diet is a lifestyle change. You wouldn't expect to exercise for a few months, tone your muscles, stop exercising and expect your muscles to remain toned. Nor, is it reasonable to expect to lose weight by restricting your calories but not expect to gain weight when you return to eating everything you want.

A lifestyle change refers to any activity or behavior in which we engage regularly to maintain our health. In the case of the CBT methods, we make a change to improve our emotional fitness. But we can't expect that fitness or change to remain intact if we don't devote attention to practice.

People have come to realize that the body needs maintenance to retain fitness and optimum health. Too often, however, people think that the brain does not require maintenance. Therefore, many people obtain initial benefits from CBT but will revert to prior thinking patterns and behaviors due to the lack of attention to the CBT methods.

A good example of what may occur is the use of relaxation methods during a time of stress. The regular use of relaxation reduces the degree of stress experienced. However, many people are likely to think "I feel good. I don't need to do this relaxation anymore." However, stopping the relaxation practice may result in a return of the symptoms associated with stress.

Unfortunately, when this occurs some people may conclude "That relaxation stuff really doesn't work!" However, that is like saying exercise doesn't work because when you stop exercise you lose muscle strength.

ERROR 4: Not Using Relaxation Regularly

A closely associated error is that many people believe they should obtain benefits from relaxation even though they use it infrequently. I can't tell you how often clients report being stressed or anxious, yet when I ask them how often they engaged in relaxation, they respond "once" or "not at all." The same clients, however, may report a very positive response from the relaxation when they use it.

Again, the regular practice of relaxation trains the brain and the body to respond differently. This practice can create a very powerful response. You may be familiar with strong automatic negative responses. For instance, if you have been very stressed at work, you may notice your body reacting with symptoms when you drive by you place of employment on your day off. Our bodies can become conditioned to stress responses and associate the stress response with a place, person, or thing.

However, our bodies can also become conditioned to the relaxation response. I had an experience once that illustrated to me just how powerful the relaxation response can be. Years ago I listened to a particular tape (before CDs and MP3s) whenever I had a stress headache. One day, years later, while I was driving and listening to the radio, my entire body suddenly relaxed. I felt an incredible, soothing peacefulness. Wondering why I suddenly felt so relaxed, I realized that one of the songs that I used to listen to was playing on the radio. My body had become conditioned to relax to that music.

To be able to experience the powerful benefits of relaxation, however, it is necessary to practice regularly.

ERROR 5: Expecting Results Without Practice.

Very closely related to the importance of using the methods regularly, is the expectation many people have that using the methods one time should be effective. In the course of my practice, I have frequently heard a client say, "I tried breathing when I was anxious and it didn't work." When I asked them how much they had practiced prior to using it for the anxiety, they have told me not at all or very little.

If you were playing baseball, would you expect to hit the ball during a game if you had never tried hitting a ball before? Of course not! However, people often believe that the techniques of CBT should be effective when they have never practiced them. I think this may be due to the techniques being very similar to other normal daily behaviors so people think that they should just be able to do it without an previous training or practice.

For example, they might think that since breathing is something they have done every day of their lives, they should be able to just slow it down at will. However, the fallacy here is that although they have been breathing their entire lives, they have not been regulating their breathing at will. These are two different things.

To put this in perspective, if I asked you to lower your body temperature (without any artificial means such as ice) you might tell me I'm crazy, that it can't be done. But your brain has regulated your body temperature all your life just as it has regulated your breathing. So why do you believe that you can't lower your body temperature? Probably because you are not as aware of it as you are of your breathing. However, it is possible to change our physiological responses such as body temperature or blood pressure but it requires advanced practice.

The point is that practice is necessary to achieve the ability to change our physiological responses. We can't expect to be proficient at calming ourselves if we never practice the techniques. In CBT, homework is everything! (I know I repeated this concept several times but it's really important!)

ERROR 6: Believing CBT is the Same as Positive Thinking.

Another common error that people make about CBT is believing that it is all about positive thinking. I have frequently heard the remark, "I've tried that positive thinking—it doesn't work." However, CBT is not about positive thinking at all. In fact, positive thinking can be just as irrational and problematic as negative thinking.

For example, if someone believes "Everything will be okay. I don't need to worry" when a catastrophe is occurring, they may not take the necessary steps to control the situation which allows it to become worse. There are times when we need to be concerned so that we can take appropriate action.

However, cognitive therapy approaches this in a realistic manner. If we are worrying about something that is not likely to occur, then we are making ourselves feel bad about something for little reason. Therefore, CBT is practical and realistic. It is about assessing our thinking so that we can take the most reasonable approach.

ERROR 7: Believing That Emotions Are Always Irrational.

Sometimes people take CBT too far and believe "If I'm completely rational, I won't feel anything." In fact, I heard Albert Ellis, one of the founding fathers of cognitive therapy, state this idea at a seminar. He said that if we are always rational, we would never be angry.

I hope I misunderstood his statement because I disagree with this concept. We are emotional beings. Emotions are an important part of our information processing system. Emotions allow us to be aware of problems that need to be addressed. So I neither believe that normal human beings can be completely free of emotions nor do I believe that it is healthy for us to not have emotions. Without emotions we can miss very important information in our environment.

For example, if you are threatened on a dark street late at night, what do you think reacts first? Do you think your emotions react first warning you of danger? Or do you intellectually assess the situation first? The initial emotional reaction prepares us to flee or to fight. The intellectual response is to determine what might be the better decision.

Certainly, our emotions can cause us to over-react. For instance, on that dark street you might feel threatened when you really aren't. And that is where CBT can help. It helps us to learn to keep our emotions in perspective and to recognize when we may be over-reacting. However, it should not be used to prevent emotions completely.

Many CBT therapists are finding standard CBT too limiting in this regard and there has been much movement to mindfulness-based CBT, often referred to as MBCT. MBCT focuses more on learning to tolerate the various emotional states through mindfulness approaches rather than trying to eliminate them. The intellectualized approach in standard CBT can be problematic for people who already have a more analytical style with avoidance of emotions.

ERROR 8: Placing Demands on Rationality

As people learn about CBT, sometimes they come to believe that if being rational is good and benefits their life, they might place a demand on themselves: "I SHOULD be completely rational all of the time."

Now, if you know anything about cognitive therapy, you know that this statement is irrational in itself for several reasons. One, is that it is a perfectionistic demand. Such demands are impossible to achieve which then causes additional distress and dysfunction. Cognitive therapy is about decreasing stress by being realistic in our expectations of ourselves.

Another reason this statement is irrational is because it is black-and-white reasoning which is the idea that if something is bad, the opposite should be good. But this isn't the case either. CBT is about finding balance whereas black-and-white thinking is about extremes. Even CBT when done to the extreme can be unhealthy.

I have often had this issue with my anxious clients. When we work on exposures to anxiety-provoking situations so that they can desensitize to the situation, they may come to believe that it is always good to challenge anxiety. In other words, if you are afraid of something, you need to face it. But that is not true because sometimes challenging a fear unnecessarily can cause more harm than good.

In particular, this attitude can cause unnecessary stress which may interfere with someone challenging the fears that are important to face. A person needs to evaluate a fear, determine in what way and how much it affects satisfaction in life, and then decide whether it needs to be dealt with. If I have a fear of snakes that doesn't really affect my life much, why should I face it? However, if it prevents me from doing something that is very important to me such as riding my bike on a wooded path, then I might choose to face it.

ERROR 9: Using CBT to Justify Not Being Responsible for Change.

Another area where people need to be cautious with CBT is using it as a justification to not change or try. Although CBT teaches a person to appreciate all aspects of themselves, it is meant to be used for building a foundation that provides a stable base from which a person can make changes.

Practitioners of CBT believe that if you feel good about yourself, you will have greater confidence to try new things and to make improvements. You are more able to acknowledge your flaws or areas in need of improvement without that acknowledgment causing you to feel bad. So we teach acceptance of yourself.

However, some people may use this concept as justification for not taking responsibility to make changes: "I am fine just the way I am." Or, they may focus on only a very specific aspect of a cognitive belief without considering the complexity of the situation. For instance, if I tell a woman "Certainly, you have the right to expect your husband to help with half the housework, but all rights come with consequences and you also need to consider the consequences of that demand and determine how it affects your marriage" I might soon hear from her husband saying that his wife told him that he should help with half the housework! She ignored the rest of the challenge to her thinking.

My point here is that CBT shouldn't be used as a justification for behavior that is unhealthy or inappropriate. It is meant to help a person examine thoughts and choices so as to improve satisfaction with life and with relationships. It is not meant to help a person to continue problematic behaviors. So even if the words are the same, it may not always mean the same thing. You need to look at the underlying meaning as well. In other words, a "should" is not always a "should." And to paraphrase Freud, "Sometimes a should is just a should (and nothing else)."

ERROR 10: Placing Demands on Mindfulness

Another frequent error is the tendency to place expectations or demands on the practice of mindfulness. The problem with this is that demands prevent the experience of mindfulness so the more we try to be mindful the less we are able to be mindful.

I experienced this years ago as a college student. During a womens' retreat, we were instructed to listen to some music to allow us to experience imagery to develop personal understanding. As I am lying on the mat and trying to allow the music to create images, I became very frustrated. I thought "I'm not having any images! Nothing is occurring! Everyone else is going to experience something and share what they are experiencing. And I have nothing! How embarrassing! This is a waste of time."

As you can see, I was not mindful at all. Of course no images occurred. I was so caught up in my (irrational) thinking that I couldn't be mindful. Finally, in frustration, I gave up. I said to myself "I don't care! I'm just going to listen to the music and not worry about trying to have any images."

As I continued to listen to the music and let all my thoughts drift away, I suddenly had one of the most powerful images that has guided my life to this day. More importantly, I learned the critical concept of not trying to be mindful. Instead of trying to be mindful, learn to allow yourself to be mindful. The more you remove the demand of mindfulness, the more you will achieve it.

Things You Should Know About Cognitive Behavioral Therapy

You've probably heard about cognitive behavioral therapy (CBT), a method of treatment based on evidence focused on changing negative thoughts and behaviours. Almost every self-help article online seems to mention it: Sleep problems? Try CBT. Trauma from childhood? Maybe CBT can help. Anxiety, depression, low self-esteem, flying fear, hangnails? CBT is your answer.

Basically, you have a good chance of receiving CBT or knowing someone you have. So what's it about? Is it really relieving psychological distress, and if so, how? How much does it cost, and can you use the techniques alone? Such details can be a mystery to the public at large. Fortunately, I'm a clinical psychologist who uses CBT in my practice, so I should be able to answer most of your questions. Now seeing the most common questions, we will do a repetition of what we have seen throughout the whole book. Let's see if you remember all the topics

1. First, what's the CBT heck?

CBT is one of a number of psychotherapy treatment methods. It is based on the assumption that many of the problems in life stem from faulty thoughts and behaviors (from which "cognitive "comes). We can alleviate distress by deliberately shifting them towards healthier, more productive goals. In practice, cognitive behavioral therapy usually involves identifying and replacing problem thoughts and behaviors with healthier responses. For example, in social situations, Jane Doe is anxious and has begun to avoid gatherings in favor of isolating evenings at home. A CBT therapist can teach her about the irrationally triggered fear response, teach her how to shift her thoughts and relax her body, and develop an action plan to help her stay calm while participating in this weekend's party. They will evaluate what worked and what didn't work next week and tweak their methods until Jane can socialize comfortably.

2. What kind of problems can CBT help and how do I know if it's right for me?

CBT is used for everything from phobia, anxiety, depression, trauma, self-esteem and ADHD to relationship problems such as poor communication or your partner's unrealistic expectations. In essence, if it's a problem involving thoughts and behaviors (which covers a lot of ground), CBT has a treatment approach. Is it okay for you? That's a hard question. Do your problems have to do with how you think and act? Do you ruminate about a previous breakup, for example, or do you find yourself mindlessly shopping online? If so, yes, you might benefit from CBT. If you are more concerned about your purpose or meaning in life, or what moments of your past color you are today, there may be other approaches that are better suited to you (and we will get to that in question #9).

3. What is the popularity of CBT?

One of the reasons why CBT is so well known and widely used is that it has been so extensively studied. Studying is a good way because it emphasizes short, direct, solution-oriented interventions. In other words, the objective is to bring about clear, measurable changes in thinking and behaviour, which is a gold mine for researchers. It also means that you can see quick results. Since a high percentage of people in our practice deal with some form of anxiety (social anxiety, anxiety about health or disease, OCD, panic, etc.), it is a central part of the work to be able to gently challenge people to confront their fears and develop new ways of relating to their own thoughts " CBT provides us with the tools to encourage people to do something very unpleasant: confront the things they avoided"

4. What's going on in a CBT session?

CBT is a form of psychotherapy, so you can expect the early sessions to be what you would see in any initial therapy sessions: Discussing payment information and cancelation policy, your therapy goals, your history and your problems review. After that, you'll talk about your struggles and try to formulate together the most effective response. In essence, the customer brings the problems they want to overcome or the situations they find stressful, and the therapist and client work together to create an action plan. An action plan means identifying problem thoughts or behaviours, finding a way to change them and developing a strategy for this change in the coming week. There's "homework "here.

5. How are CBT homework?

CBT focuses on providing rapid (8 to 12 sessions, which are rapid according to therapeutic standards) and effective symptom reduction, which is best done throughout the week, not just during the therapy session. Typical homework may include relaxation exercises, keeping a journal of thoughts and emotions throughout the week, using worksheets that target a particular area of growth, reading a book that addresses your problems, or looking for situations to apply your new approach. For example, Jane may want to keep an eye on meet-up events that challenge her to overcome her fears while applying her new techniques for relaxation. Another example: Let's say that his negative internal self-talk is a major factor in John Doe 's depression-he constantly lowers himself on a loop. John and his CBT therapist can talk about a technique called "stop thinking, "in which he abruptly disrupts the flow of negative thoughts by yelling (in his mind) "stop! " as he turns his thoughts to something more positive, such as an affirmation or a meditation app. Homework can involve at least once every day practicing this technique until the next session. In the next session, John and his therapist will debrief, assess what worked and what didn't work, and tweak the process for the next week.

6. How long does CBT usually last?

One of CBT 's highlights is that it focuses on eliminating symptoms as quickly as possible, usually in a couple of weeks or months. Of course, people rarely have only one problem to work on in therapy, so this length depends on the number and severity of the problems, but briefness is essential for this approach. This leads to one of the main differences between CBT and many other forms of treatment. One of CBT 's founders, Donald Meichenbaum, says, "[We ask] what questions and how. While other treatment approaches spend a lot of time digging deeply and asking why you feel depressed, anxious or low self-esteem, CBT adheres to current thoughts and behaviors. CBT focuses on helping you reduce your fear rather than examining why you are afraid of snakes. While some people are happy to reduce their symptoms, others want to know why they first exist. Deeper approaches such as psychodynamic therapy may be more satisfactory for them.

7. Can people use CBT techniques outside of actual therapy sessions?

Did you ever keep a journal of gratitude? What about your donut intake monitoring? Did you track your daily steps or check your sleep? Then you're using some of CBT 's principles in your daily life. Many others CBT techniques can be found in books such as David Burns ' Feeling Good or Edmund Bourne 's Anxiety and Phobia Workbook, online, or in popular applications such as Headspace and Happify. But a period of time in structured therapy is still the best approach for a CBT course tailored to you and your problems.

8. How much does CBT cost and is it covered by insurance?

CBT is psychotherapy, so if your insurance covers psychotherapy or behavioral medicine, most, if not all, of your CBT treatment should be covered. If you pay out of the pocket, the cost of CBT ranges from free or sliding in some community clinics to $200 + per session in a private practice. Once again, the time someone spends on treatment is usually less than other treatment approaches, so it can be cheaper in the long run. On a therapist finder website such as Psychology Today or Good Therapy, you can search for a therapist who practices CBT and fits your budget.

9. Are there any sides to choose CBT compared to another type of treatment?

Some clients may feel that therapy is a place where they come and process their experiences with their therapist's gentle facilitation. Their main objective may not be to deal with a particular symptom or problem habit, but rather with general growth and a long-term relationship with a therapist. They may want to explore their memories, dreams and early relationships with their therapist's guidance. Since CBT can be a more direct and practical therapy style, it may not be helpful for someone who is looking for this kind of profound, relationship work. However, many qualified CBT therapists are very flexible in their approach and can adapt to the needs of a variety of clients. As Dr. Hsia admits, CBT is not without its criticisms. " CBT 's fair criticism highlights its assumptions about what helps people get better, "he says. Again, CBT focuses on symptoms rather than the deeper roots of these symptoms, and some psychologists who feel that the deeper roots are essential would consider CBT to be short-sighted. In the end, you have to find out what works best for you, which may take some trial and mistake. It may be helpful to talk to your therapist (or potential therapist) about what you are looking for and ask them how they approach the treatment. Whether you are receiving CBT treatment or another method, the most important thing is that you feel a safe, confident relationship with your therapist and that the treatment makes sense for you.

Pros & Cons of CBT Therapy

There is always a risk that bad feelings will return, but it should be easier for you to control them with your CBT skills. This is why it is important to continue to practice your CBT skills even after you feel better and have completed your sessions. CBT may not, however, be successful or appropriate for everyone.

Below are some of the advantages and disadvantages of the approach.

The benefits of CBT

In cases where the patient does not see an improvement with medication alone, cognitive behavioral therapy is effective. It does not take as long as other types of treatment. Cognitive behavioral therapy is also structured in such a way that it can be offered in different formats, including group therapy, self-help books and online programmes. Most people receive cognitive behavioral treatment because it teaches them practical strategies that can be applied to everyday life. It offers patients solutions to improve their minds every day.

Below are some specific benefits of CBT;

• can be as effective as medication in the treatment of certain mental health disorders and

• can be helpful in cases where medication alone has not worked. Compared to other speech therapies, it can be completed in a relatively short time.

• Focus on retraining your thoughts and changing behaviors to change your feelings. CBT 's highly structured nature means that it can be provided in various formats, including in groups, self-help books and computer programs.

• The skills you learn in CBT are useful, practical and helpful strategies that can be incorporated into everyday life to help you better cope with future stresses and difficulties even after treatment is complete.

CBT 's disadvantages

First of all, a high level of commitment is required for cognitive behavioral therapy. If you don't cooperate, your therapist can't help you. If you have a busy lifestyle, the frequency of cognitive behavioral therapy sessions may be a challenge. In addition, it may not be a good choice for people with complex mental problems or learning difficulties due to the highly structured nature of cognitive behavioral therapy. Many people fear cognitive behavioral treatment because it forces them to face their root of anxiety.

You should be prepared for an initial period of fear and discomfort if you choose this type of therapy. Another significant disadvantage is that cognitive behavioral therapy does not address other problems, such as families and social factors, that can have a significant impact on the patient. It is not suitable for everyone, however effective cognitive behavioral therapy is. Although it can work wonderful things for your friends, you may not benefit from it. In addition, cognitive behavioral therapy tends to focus instead of the cause on the specific problem. The therapy focuses on the identification of current problems rather than past problems. Someone with a mental condition resulting from childhood trauma, for example, may not see much improvement in cognitive behavioral therapy.

Below are some specific disadvantages of CBT;

• To take advantage of CBT, you must commit to the process. A therapist can help and advise you, but without your cooperation, you can't get rid of your problems.

• It can take a lot of your time to attend regular CBT sessions and perform any additional work between sessions.

• It may not be appropriate for people with more complex mental health needs or learning difficulties due to the structured nature of CBT.

• Since CBT can confront your emotions and anxieties, you may experience initial periods of anxiety or emotional discomfort.

• Some critics argue that CBT does not address the possible underlying causes of mental health conditions, such as an unhappy childhood, because it only addresses current problems and focuses on specific issues.

• CBT focuses on the ability of the individual to change himself (his thoughts, feelings and behaviors) and does not address broader problems in systems or families that often have a significant impact on the health and well-being of an individual.

COGNITIVE
BEHAVIORAL THERAPY
MADE SIMPLE

By

Daniel Anderson

TABLE OF CONTENTS

INTRODUCTION

We must have all experienced our hearts pounding very fast before a major job interview or when we are asked to make a speech before important personalities. We worry over family and financial problems or feel jittery at the prospect of meeting a date for the first time. If your worries and fears are preventing you from living your life in a normal way, you may very well be suffering from an anxiety disorder. Here we want to show you simple techniques you can use to prevent and overcome anxiety. These techniques have been reported as indeed panic attacks and anxiety cures.

You are free to take the techniques seriously and stop swallowing dangerous panic attacks medication in order to completely eliminate panic attacks from your life. I was once an anxiety and panic attacks sufferer. I missed several important job interviews because of this problem until I was able to find a permanent cure using the One Move technique. Before I used the One Move technique to cure my panic attacks and anxiety, these were the techniques - cognitive behavioral therapy and graded exposure therapy - that helped me overcome anxiety and panic attacks.

Cognitive behavioral therapy and graded exposure

therapy are the two effective anxiety and panic attacks treatment techniques. The two techniques are actually behavioral therapy and they focus on behavioral modifications rather than on underlying psychological problems of the past. The two techniques took me between 5 and 20 weekly sessions.

Cognitive behavior therapy - focuses on your thoughts and behavior modifications. When used in panic attacks anxiety cures, cognitive behavioral therapy helped me identify and challenge the negative thinking patterns and irrational beliefs that are fueling my anxiety and panic attacks.

Graded exposure therapy - This technique helped me to confront my fears in a safe and controlled manner. Through repeated and graded exposures to the feared situations, I was able to acquire a greater sense of control of myself. As I was being made to face my fears without being harmed, my anxiety and panic attacks gradually disappeared.

I believe strongly that these techniques are the best approach to treating and eliminating the twin problems of anxiety and panic attacks. Even the medical world now agrees that the best treatment for anxiety disorder is through behavioral therapy. The One Move technique is an advanced from of behavioral therapy which I used to completely cure all my symptoms. This is a heart-warming news to all sufferers. Your panic attacks and anxiety can be cured without costly and dangerous antidepressant medications.

Feel confident and beautiful once more. Experience for yourself the immediate and fast cure for panic attacks and anxiety with the One Move technique.

How do you overcome Anxiety?

Steps to Overcoming Anxiety

With the aid of the lists below, you can successfully overcome anxiety;

Overcoming anxiety after it's developed into a major difficulty in your life can often be confusing and upsetting. However, anxiety disorders are very treatable problems.

This is a consumer guide for people who seek anxiety relief, but don't know how to get there. However, I suggest that everyone who seeks relief from chronic anxiety should review these steps, and complete any which you haven't yet done.

Step One:

Learn a little about anxiety disorders

Understanding how anxiety "works" is one of the keys to overcoming anxiety. Read my description of the different anxiety disorders and compare your experience with those descriptions.

Use the book to learn more about overcoming anxiety disorders. The purpose here is not to self-diagnose yourself - please consult a licensed clinician for a diagnosis - but to inform yourself as much as possible before you consult a clinician so that you can evaluate what a clinician tells you, be an informed consumer, and find effective methods for overcoming anxiety.

The internet is full of anxiety scams, so be wary! When something sounds too good to be true, it probably is.

It's common to experience some depression along with an anxiety disorder, and this is often a source of confusion to people. If this sounds relevant to you, read a little bit about depression.

Step Two:

Consult with your primary physician

A consultation with your physician is a must if you suspect you have panic attacks or generalized anxiety.

These symptoms can be caused by a variety of physiological disorders, and you should rule them out as part of the diagnostic process. You should certainly have one complete physical after the onset of these symptoms.

The other anxiety disorders don't generally require a physical, because there isn't any reason to think that they are caused by another physical ailment. However, you might still want to consult your physician, especially if you have a long history with that person. You might want his/her opinion about your situation; you might want a referral; or you might want to find out about possible medications you could use.

Be aware, however, that most physicians, because they specialize in various aspects of physical health, have very little training in the area of anxiety disorders. What training they do have, with respect to overcoming anxiety, is usually limited to medications. They may often be surprisingly unaware of cognitive behavioral treatment for anxiety disorders, even though it is generally regarded as the treatment of choice. When it comes time to seek professional help for overcoming anxiety disorders, you will probably need to go elsewhere.

If you don't have panic attacks or generalized anxiety, and have no other reason to consult your physician about overcoming anxiety, then skip ahead to Step Three.

Before you call for an appointment, make some written notes of what you want to discuss with your physician. The doctor's staff will probably ask you why you want an appointment; tell them that you've been having some problems and summarize them, briefly.

Many people have a fear of doctors, and have trouble making an appointment. This is a phobia, and will generally respond to the same CBT approach, once you decide that a visit to the doctor, however anxiety provoking, is in your best interest.

What to Expect from Your Physician

Your physician should listen to your symptoms, review your history, ask questions, and offer feedback and recommendations for overcoming anxiety. Since most physicians are trained principally in physical health and medicine, there is no reason to expect him/her to be an expert in anxiety disorders. However, your physician should take your complaints seriously, evaluate them, and offer suggestions for finding additional help.

If you are having panic attacks and have never been tested for thyroid malfunction, for instance, you should receive such a test, because thyroid problems can sometimes cause a person to have panic-like symptoms. If your symptoms resemble those associated with mitral valve prolapse, you should probably have an echocardiogram to evaluate that possibility. There are numerous physical conditions which can produce panic symptoms, and your physician should evaluate you for those possibilities if that has never been done before.

However, if you have had those tests before, and your doctor assured you that you were in good health, do not push for continual retesting! Many people do this because they hate the idea that they may have an anxiety disorder, and instead hope to find a physical problem. You can waste lots of time and money this way.

One set of tests is generally enough. If you need a second opinion for a particular reason, then get one. If you get more than two sets of tests, seriously consider the possibility that you are getting diverted from your task of overcoming anxiety!

Let's suppose that you've had a good consultation with your physician, the appropriate tests have ruled out any physical ailments which could be causing your symptoms, and you want to get professional help with overcoming anxiety. Now you're ready for step three.

Step Three:

Learn about the available treatments

There are basically two kinds of treatment which clinical research has shown to be effective in overcoming anxiety disorders: cognitive behavioral treatment (CBT) and certain forms of medication. Other forms of psychotherapy are often helpful in resolving some of the issues associated with anxiety disorders, but are generally not regarded as capable of resolving the primary problem. Which form of treatment should you choose?

My view is that most people with anxiety disorders are best served by trying a cognitive behavioral treatment first, and seeing what kind of results you get from that. You can always try medication later, if the CBT doesn't provide all the results you seek.

There are three principal reasons to try CBT first. First, unlike medication, CBT has no side effects. Second, the use of medications tends to lead a person to believe that he or she is now "protected" from anxiety disorders, and the sense of being protected often leads an anxiety sufferer to feel more vulnerable in the long run. Third, the results you get from CBT treatment will generally be much more long lasting than those you get from medications. Results from medication treatments tend to fade after the medications are withdrawn.

Some patients will need medication in addition to CBT, and some will not, depending on the severity of their condition and their particular diagnosis. Medication is nothing to be avoided if it seems necessary. However, I do believe it's true that in our culture, medications are overprescribed for these problems. This can be avoided if you start with CBT first.

The Anxiety Disorders Association of America

website includes an overview of medications used to treat anxiety disorders

There are new forms of CBT in development, often labeled as "Third Wave" therapies. One in particular, Acceptance and Commitment Therapy (ACT) is quite useful in the treatment of Panic Disorder and other anxiety disorders. In my work, I blend methods from both traditional CBT and ACT, and find them both very useful in overcoming anxiety disorders.

Do I Need "Treatment" at All?

You may be wondering if you really need to see a professional, or if you can't just solve this problem on your own. In general, the more difficulty you are having, the more you may need professional help, but only you can decide how urgent your need is. Certainly there are many good sources of self help information you can use in overcoming anxiety disorders. If you choose to try anxiety self help, I suggest you follow a few guidelines.

* Get a "buddy", a coach, or a support person, with whom you can discuss your efforts on a regular basis. They don't have to be an expert. A major benefit is that, by telling someone of your efforts, you will find it easier to monitor your progress and hold yourself accountable. It's easy to forget about all your good intentions when you keep them to yourself.

* Follow an organized plan. Find a good self help book which pertains to your problem, and make that the basis of your work. If you have panic attacks and like the approach you find on this website, then try my Panic Attacks Workbook. If your problem is more about chronic worry, take a look at my book for chronic worriers, The Worry Trick.

* Evaluate your progress at regular intervals, at least monthly. After six months, re-evaluate your progress. If you're satisfied you're making reasonable progress toward overcoming anxiety, continue on course. If you're not, consider seeking professional help at that time.

What about Group Treatment for overcoming anxiety?

Among the advantages of group treatment for overcoming anxiety are lower cost and the opportunity to share experiences with others who can relate to your situation. This can be particularly important for people who feel especially ashamed and imagine that they are one of a very few who suffer in this way.

I don't really think there are any disadvantages to a well run group treatment, although many people shy away from it because they believe they would pick up more fears from hearing other people's problems. In my experience in running groups, this has not been a problem and, while people are usually quite nervous before the first meeting, their anxiety is usually much lower by the end of the meeting.

Group treatments are often not available, so consider yourself fortunate if they are offered in your area. Your own personal preference is probably the most important deciding factor in the choice between group and individual treatment.

...And Support Groups?

You may also find it helpful to attend a support group. There are general purpose support groups designed to help people with a variety of psychological problems, and there are anxiety support groups which have a more specific focus - anxiety problems in general, or specific anxiety disorders such as Panic Disorder, Obsessive Compulsive Disorder, etc.

I think most people with a clearly defined anxiety disorder are better served by a support group which focuses specifically on their kind of problem, if such a group is available. However, there are also some good "general purpose" groups, such as Recovery International.

Step Four:

Identify Qualified Therapists

If you decide to get professional help, be prepared to do some work to find a good therapist. You can start by getting the names of therapists in your area who offer the kind of treatment you seek. The websites of the Anxiety Disorders Association of America and the Association for Behavioral and Cognitive Therapies offer a "therapist finder" section to help you find a specialist in your area. The sites for the Obsessive Compulsive Foundation and the TLC Foundation (compulsive behaviors such as hair pulling, skin picking, and nail biting) offer similar lists of professionals who specialize in those areas.

You will probably be better off if you can find a therapist who has specialized training and experience with the anxiety disorder for which you seek help. However, be aware that these lists will generally include any therapist who wishes to be included; they are not a licensing or accreditation process, simply a place to start. You still need to be an informed consumer.

Step Five:

Select a Therapist and Begin Treatment

An initial evaluation with a therapist may take anywhere from one to two sessions. It should enable the therapist to learn enough about you to give you some feedback about your situation and how that therapist proposes to help you, and should also give you a chance to ask more questions. One area you should certainly discuss with the therapist is what to expect in treatment, i.e., how will you know it is working? What would be a sign that it is not working?

You will probably also want to know how long treatment will take. What I tell new patients is that, while I can't immediately predict how long their particular situation will require, I do expect that they will have a gut feeling that we are moving in the right direction within the first month of weekly sessions, and that they should see some progress within the first two months. If this doesn't happen, it's a sign that something isn't working right, and we should figure out what's wrong.

CHAPTER ONE

COGNITIVE BEHAVIORAL THERAPY

The brain is a fascinating, time-saving beast. It has fast-tracked responses to certain situations so you don't even have to think about reacting, you just do. This becomes a problem, though, when your automatic response is one of fear in situations where, in reality, there's nothing to be afraid of.

It could be that you go into a state of panic every time you're called in to a meeting with your boss, because years ago, you lost your job in a similar way. Maybe you constantly overreact to innocuous comments from your other half, because you're scared they're going to leave you the same way your ex did. Or it could be that walking to the bus stop is riddled with anxiety thanks to your neighbour's Great Dane, which you believe will one day escape and attack you.

If you're tired of feeling this way, scientists say you can retrain the part of the brain that's responsible for this reaction. It's called the amygdala, and it's an almond-shaped collection of neurons located in each side lobe of the brain.

"It's a part of the brain that occurs in animals and

163

humans," Dr Fiona Kumfor, research officer at Neuroscience Research Australia, says. "So it's not this high level cognitive process that we associate with being human in terms of reasoning and thinking rationally. The amygdala is a very automatic part of the brain that helps us respond to our environment and it seems to be important for registering emotional information."

The brain is primed to quickly identify emotional stimuli, especially when we're in a dangerous situation, so that we can then act fast. "But in a modern lifestyle we're not really being confronted with tigers that we need to run away from". "Instead, it might be stress from work, or that you're never fully relaxed, and your body can then be in this hyper-aroused state where the amygdala is overworking. You might be interpreting emotional cues in the environment in a more exaggerated sense than needed."

Luckily, the brain is plastic and can be retrained. "Potentially, if we can retrain the amygdala, we can regulate these emotions so they're deployed in appropriate situations and not impacting on everyday life and mental health," Kumfor adds.

Shrinking the amygdala

A regular meditation practice of 30 minutes a day has been shown to reduce the size of the amygdala, allowing your rational thinking brain to take over, according to neuroscientists at Harvard University in the US. But which meditation is best? Associate psychologist David R Vago, from the Functional Neuroimaging Laboratory at Harvard Medical School, is an expert in the neuroscience of mindfulness. There are three practices that are best for a sustainable healthy mind.

The first is 'focused attention', where you concentrate on a single object, like a sound, the breath or how your body feels. The second is 'open monitoring', in which you become aware of your thoughts (see our example, right). The third is 'loving kindness', a traditional Buddhist practice in which you cultivate compassion – even for people you don't really like.

To try one of these approaches, do a search online for a guided meditation. Start small with only five minutes a day and slowly increase your practice time.

Unlearning the fear response

Another way to retrain the amygdala is through exposure therapy. As the amygdala is associated with fear, this approach can help those with anxiety, phobias, chronic pain or post-traumatic stress disorder, Dr Sylvia Gustin, senior neuroscientist at

Neuroscience Research Australia, says. "In this technique we develop a fear hierarchy, which you then gradually work through to the most fearful situation," she explains.

The way it works is you list all the things that trigger your anxiety, then rank them in order of least to most unnerving. Rather than avoiding all these situations (which would mean the amygdala isn't retrained so it remains overstimulated) you start by exposing yourself to the smallest trigger. Once you're comfortable with that, you work your way up the list so that you can unlearn the fear response.

Quietening the anxiety

When therapy is combined with mindfulness, it can have even better results. A small-scale US study of war veterans with post-traumatic stress disorder found that those who completed group therapy along with mindfulness training showed a shift in their brain activity. The University of Michigan Medical School researchers found the areas of the brain in the regions that dealt with threats, including the amygdala, weren't as active as they previously were.

Gustin is also an advocate of mindful practices, like yoga, to help decrease the activity of the amygdala, but acknowledges that strong anxiety can make it hard to focus. In those cases she says to be patient and stick with it: "We only heal ourselves when we treat ourselves nicely."

Do this daily

Psychotherapist Dr Timothy Stokes says this 'open monitoring' practice is ideal for retraining the amygdala: "The most powerful therapeutic tools begin with observing our thoughts and feelings. This practice creates an observer who watches and allays the tendency to get hijacked by problematic thoughts and feelings."

1. Imagine a situation that causes you anxiety or usually leads to you losing your cool, making the image as vivid as possible.

2. Pay attention to the emotions this causes. It could be an unsettled stomach, a sad feeling in your chest or a burning feeling in your torso.

3. Say to yourself: "This energy is just a feeling in my body."

4. Repeat steps one to three for up to 30 minutes.

4 things to do when anxiety strikes

Follow these steps from meditation expert and Zen teacher Diane Musho Hamilton...

1. Stay present Notice how your body is responding to the situation or perceived threat you're encountering.

2. Let go of the story Empty the mind of thoughts and

judgement. This will break the loop between the mind and body.

3. Focus Is part of your body tight, shaking or painful? Focus on these sensations without trying to control or change them.

4. Breathe Aim for a consistent series of rhythmic, smooth and even breaths. This will allow you to centre yourself.

Still anxious? Try this…

Tapping

Tap your temples, cheeks or shoulders repeatedly until you calm down. The mild brain stimulation from the tapping helps to erase the physical basis for a fear memory in the amygdala, a study published in the journal Traumatology found. It doesn't matter if you tap one side or both. You can also try this the day before a stressful event.

Basking in blue

Picture the amygdala inside your skull. Now imagine it's glowing with soft blue light. Visualise the healing light pouring into your frontal lobes and gently setting off billions of neural pathways. This should help you better control your response to the situation that's causing the panic and foster a sense of calm.

Imagining a feather

Close your eyes and use your mind's eye to imagine a feather gently tickling the surface of your amygdala. This will help minimise the fear or anxiety you're feeling and stimulate a series of positive responses from the brain instead.

Proven Tricks For Overcoming Anxiety And Fear

Back in the earlier days of evolution, humans were prey to giant hyenas, cave bears, and predatory kangaroos.

We've been able to outlast those guys, but evolutionary psychologists will tell you that we're still on constant lookout for the thing that wants to eat us next.

The trouble is, the audience at your next presentation is not, in fact, a bunch of razor-toothed animals. They generally want to see you do well.

Since being plagued by anxiety is a sure way to sabotage your own success, we've put together a collection of research-backed tips for overcoming your fears.

Breathe deeply because it lets your nervous system know that it can chill out.

You've probably heard that breathing is a good call if

you're stressed out.

But what's fascinating is the reason why it works so well.

"Deep diaphragmatic breathing is a powerful anxiety-reducing technique because it activates the body's relaxation response," explains Psych Central editor Margarita Tartakovsky. "It helps the body go from the fight-or-flight response of the sympathetic nervous system to the relaxed response of the parasympathetic nervous system."

Slowly expose yourself to the things you're afraid of, so they're no longer unfamiliar to you.

If you're trying to get comfortable with negotiating, speaking in public, or other scary activities, psychologists often recommend exposure therapy.

Rehab Institute of Chicago neuroscientist Katherina Hauner has found that it can dramatically improve the way people relate to their fears.

"It is usually done in a series of hierarchical steps, starting with a relatively low level of engagement with the feared situation, and increasing the level with each step," she told the Huffington Post.

"For exposure therapy with a dog phobia," she says, "we might start with just looking at a very small puppy from many feet away, and eventually work our way up to petting a very large dog."

Recognize when you're succumbing to 'misplaced' anxiety, and let it go.

As Wharton research scholar Jeremy Yip has found, fear about one thing in your life has a way of spilling over into other parts of your life.

If you have car trouble on your way to work, there's a good chance that feeling of anxiety will carry over into your workday.

You might feel less confident about pitching your boss on a new project because when you ask yourself, "How do I feel about this?" your general feelings of anxiety make you more risk-averse.

To deal with that, try and recognize where the fear is coming from. If you're worried because you need to make improvements, listen to that. If you're worried because your exhaust is making funny noises, don't.

Spend time with your friends — social support reduces anxiety.

Three decades of research shows that people with close friends are better able to survive divorces, job losses, and other traumatic events.

"Friendfluence" author Carlin Flora says that friendship has long been an evolutionary advantage.

"When we lived in groups where survival itself was difficult, you needed someone who would be guaranteed to throw you a lifeline," she told Thought Catalog. "You can easily theorize that the notion of a best friend developed because we needed someone where we were number one on their list and they were number one on our list in those life and death situations."

Exercise to protect yourself against the effects of stress, which include anxiety and fear.

Working out helps people feel better.

The Mayo Clinic says that exercise helps release anxiety in three main ways:

• Exercise releases brain chemicals associated with easing depression, like endorphins.

• Exercise enhances your immune system, lessening the chance of depression.

• Exercise increases body temperature, which helps people calm down.

And a pro tip: If you're new to working out, psychologists say that "taking away the choice" of whether you're going exercise is the key to sticking to a workout plan.

Reframe anxiety as excitement so that you can devote more energy and resources to the situation.

Harvard Business School assistant professor Alison Wood Brooks has found that the best way to work with anxiety isn't to keep calm — but to get excited.

Emotions happen at two levels: There's the physical sensation, called arousal in the psych world, and then the way you mentally interpret it, called valence.

When you're anxious, your heart rate goes up — that's high arousal. And you read it as bad news — that's a negative valence.

The takeaway: If you're anxious, reframe it as excitement, since you can stay in that high arousal state but read it as good news instead. In experiments, that tactic makes people better public speakers and karaoke singers.

Prevent yourself from always focusing on the negatives by looking at the big picture.

Here's a simple, age-old exercise from Swiss psychiatrist Paul Dubois. Every night, grab a piece of paper and draw two columns. List the things that troubled you in one, and things that were favorable in the other. Make at least one favorable entry for each troubling one.

The realization that you have good things happening every day helps prevent you from just thinking about the negatives.

A few times every day, recognize that at this very moment you're doing OK.

Neurospsychologist Rick Hanson says in his Psychology Today column that our humaninstincts of survival make us constantly unsettled and fearful, protecting us against ever completely letting our guard down.

But it's all a lie, according to Hanson. Your brain is automatically telling you something bad is going to happen, which may be true in the future, but not right now. By reminding yourself that you're OK right now, you can more easily settle your fear and build well-being.

Realize that not everything is the end of the world; one way to do this is by consciously trivializing tasks.

Social psychologist Susan K. Perry suggests in her Psychology Today column that you always think of yourself as playing. If something goes wrong, you can just try again, or try it in some other way.

And when you compare something in your daily life to decisions that are truly life-and-death, it gives you better perspective as to what's really important — and that failure at something that's probably just trivial isn't something to be so fearful or anxious about.

CHAPTER TWO

EXERCISES DESIGNED TO DEAL WITH ANXIETY

How a person deals with other human beings is a big factor in whether or not he or she succeeds in business and life. It involves emotional intelligence (EI), or the ability to recognize and appropriately react to feelings in yourself and the people around you, particularly when it comes to handling stress and frustration. According to Gustavo Oliveira--a consultant who has helped about 2,000 people worldwide improve their EI using something called The DeRose Method--it's a skill everyone can sharpen. Here are his words on four ways to build your emotional intelligence.

Study yourself.

To get a better understanding of your emotional responses, behaviors, and where your weaknesses may lie, learn to pay attention to your reactions and behaviors. And ask people close to you--only if they'll be honest--to tell you what areas of your personality need work.

Manage emotions during stressful situations by breathing correctly.

Deep and steady breathing through the nose with a relaxed ribcage is one of the best ways to lower stress in the body, and strong medicine for anxiety, fear and anger. Deep breathing sends a message to your brain to calm down and relax. The brain then sends this message to your body, resulting in a lower heart rate and blood pressure. And when you are relaxed and calm you can better manage your immediate emotions.

Channel your emotions.

One powerful method of handling negative emotions is to transform negative energies into positive ones by redirecting them to fuel new opportunities. For example, in 2009 I was expanding two successful businesses. Two years later, both had failed and my money was gone. I was crushed, frustrated and disappointed, but instead of letting my emotions reinforce an unproductive mindset and behaviors, I took a five-hour drive and started thinking about ways I could channel the power of frustration into something positive. During this time, I realized that my failures actually taught me many valuable lessons on how to run a business and the things that must be avoided. I decided to teach these lessons to others and created a course which was a huge success and became an amazing new asset.

Transmute your emotions.

Try to transform negative feelings such as anger,

hatred, pain, and jealousy into positive ones such as, love, admiration, compassion and kindness. For example, I had a student who was a professional stand-up paddle (SUP) athlete and would become emotionally unstable every time a competitor provoked him during competitions, which would negatively impact his performance. So, I created a behavioral training response for him: I asked him to smile at the competitor, row harder and intensify his focus. With time and training his response improved drastically and his new and unexpected behavior destabilized the competitors who provoked him.

Envy is another common negative emotion. Some of my students have admitted that the achievements of others make them feel as though if they are not good enough. I train them to transform the feeling and substitute it with admiration for the person's success. They come to see it as an opportunity to learn from the person's strengths, which is a more useful and productive response.

Anxiety Disorders Treatment - Phobias

Most anxiety disorders are readily treatable with a combination of psychotherapy and medication. Learn the details of these treatments and other treatment options for generalized anxiety disorder, panic disorder, agoraphobia, social phobia, specific phobia, and post-traumatic stress disorder/acute stress disorder. Treatments for anxiety depend upon the specific disorder diagnosed by a trained mental health professional. Below you will find some general treatment guidelines for different Anxiety Disorders.

This document deals with the treatment of Phobias (fears). Other available documents deal with the treatment of Panic-Related Anxiety (including Agoraphobia), Trauma and Generalized Anxiety

Social Phobia

Social phobia is the most common anxiety disorder in the population. Both men and women experience it equally. The greatest single fear that exists for people is the fear of giving a public presentation or talk, which is a symptom of social phobia. This is because at the root of social phobia is the excessive fear of either being scrutinized by others or of performing a behavior out of anxiety in front of others that might be embarrassing or humiliating, such as speaking unclearly, trembling, or even blushing.

For those suffering from social phobia it can greatly affect the quality of their lives. Oftentimes, because of the extreme anxiety those with social phobia experience during interactions with others, they avoid many social opportunities. Some have had their career potential significantly thwarted if their career advancement has rested upon giving public presentations or developing career networking relationships. Others with social phobia struggle with feelings of loneliness because their social anxiety gets in the way of pursuing dating opportunities or they may avoid social gatherings such as parties.

Social phobia can often be confused with shyness. However, for the majority of those suffering with social phobia they tend not to be shy around those they are familiar with; they can even be quite outgoing when there is not the fear of making an impression on someone whose opinion of them is unknown. Also, those with social phobia experience an extremely high level of anxiety in social situations that far exceeds the discomfort that shy people experience in social situations.

Up until recently, not much was known or understood about social phobia, especially in terms of how to treat it. We now know that people who suffer from social phobia tend to misinterpret neutral social clues so that they think others are negatively evaluating them. They are also very concerned with making a positive impression on people because they greatly desire approval from others. They often doubt their own abilities to be able to be successful in making a good impression. Fortunately, we now have effective therapy interventions to treat those with social phobia.

Psychotherapy

The treatment of choice for social phobia is cognitive behavioral therapy within a group setting called CBGT (cognitive behavioral group therapy). The ideal treatment group size for CBGT includes six patients and two therapists. This treatment relies on a triad of cognitive behavioral interventions, which include: simulated exposures to feared situations through role-plays, cognitive restructuring, and homework assignments done in in vivo exposure.

Before group treatment begins, the patient meets with the therapist and a rank-ordered hierarchy of the patient's most to least feared social situations is constructed. The group creates simulated scenarios in which the patient is exposed to his/her least feared social situations and as the patient is able to conquer these scenarios, moves up on his/her hierarchy list. If the patient begins to feel anxious or increased physiological arousal during a simulated situation, the patient is taught to use a variety of relaxation techniques, such as deep breathing to reduce the anxiety. It is through these simulated exposures that patients are able to face their fears and work through them in a monitored, safe setting.

The second component of CBGT is cognitive therapy. This is very effective since researchers have discovered that social phobia is largely born out of irrational beliefs that people develop over time. The cognitive beliefs of someone with social phobia are based upon the possibility of being negatively evaluated by others, which leads to strong feelings of vulnerability. Also, because those with social phobia tend to have a strong need for approval from others, they fear that they lack the self-esteem, social skills, or ability to make a good social impression on people.

During the first few sessions of CBGT the therapist educates the patients about cognitive therapy and how they can learn to replace their irrational beliefs that lead to anxiety or fear with healthy beliefs. Throughout the simulated scenarios, the group members can then challenge each other's irrational beliefs. By being able to point out to a group member during a simulated exposure that the member's self-perception about how they are coming across in a social situation is distorted, it offers important cognitive restructuring in the moment. CBGT is a careful balancing act between exposure and periods of cognitive restructuring.

The third component of CBGT is having the patients carry out in vivo homework assignments. This means that once the patient has mastered a feared scenario in the group setting, that the patient then goes and exposes himself/herself to a real-life similarly feared scenario, such as giving a presentation or going to a party. This allows for the skills that the patient learns in the group to be transferred to real-life situations.

There are many advantages that the group setting offers to those suffering from social phobia as compared to receiving individual therapy. First, those with various degrees of social phobia can learn vicariously through each other how to effectively handle their fears in social situations. Second, it helps group participants to realize that there are other people with similar fears and problems. This realization helps to reduce participants' fears that their problems are unique and mysterious. Third, by participating in a group treatment it helps to strengthen the patient's public commitment to change. Fourth, a group offers multiple partners with whom role-plays can be practiced. Fifth, a group offers a range of participants who can provide invaluable feedback to each other to help challenge the participant's irrational beliefs underlying their anxiety.

Since a person with social phobia has usually been struggling with the disorder for many years, 3 months of CBGT is not going to completely rid a person of social phobia; however, a reduction in the patient's symptoms should be evident. If after the twelve weeks of CBGT the patient's social phobia has not improved, then it is recommended that the patient continue either in another CBGT group and/or receive individualized psychotherapy treatment. If the person's anxiety within the feared social situations is severe enough to produce panic attacks, then panic control techniques and education about panic attacks should supplement the person's treatment. (See treatment for panic disorder). If the person really does have weak social skills, then social skills training as a supplemental treatment intervention would be quite helpful. Another treatment alternative to try after engaging in CBGT is psychotropic medication.

Medication

Medication for social phobia should be considered as a second line treatment after effective cognitive behavioral treatment has been attempted. Some medications can be helpful in the treatment of someone with social phobia in which cognitive behavioral therapy has been unsuccessful. The medications that have proven to be most successful in treating social phobia are the antidepressant medications called MAOIs (monoamine oxidase inhibitors), such as phenelzine (Nardil). The MAOIs seem to work best for generalized social fears. However, taking MAOIs requires many dietary restrictions because certain foods containing the pressor amine, Tyramine, such as the majority of cheeses, alcoholic beverages, and yeast products can produce an adverse reaction with the medication causing dangerously high blood pressure.

For more specific forms of social phobia such as

public speaking and performance anxiety the beta-blockers, such as atenolol have been successful. These provide the convenience of only having to take them just a few hours before the specific anxiety provoking event. However, these medications have not proven to be very successful for severe generalized social phobia.

Recently, the SSRI anti-depressant medication called Paroxetine (Paxil) has received attention for reducing the symptoms of social phobia. This medication generally has few side effects and can be taken for more severe generalized forms of social phobia.

Specific Phobia

Specific phobias are the most prevalent anxiety disorders within the population. They occur when a person develops an irrational fear to a specified object or situation and feels a great degree of anxiety or even has a panic attack when exposed to that feared object or situation. Approximately five to twelve percent of the population has a specific phobia with slightly more women than men being affected by a phobia. Phobias that develop during childhood are usually outgrown by adolescence. Most specific phobias develop during adolescence or adulthood in a person's mid-twenties.

A phobia can develop in a person at anytime as a reaction to a traumatic incident. For example, if a person is in an accident that occurs on a bridge the experience may create a phobia of bridges. Sometimes people can develop a phobia by witnessing something bad happening to another person. For example, witnessing a person being bitten by a snake might create a phobia of snakes in the person who witnessed the incident. People can also develop phobias from hearing about information that might frighten them, such as a person who hears an in-depth story about a plane crash on the news might then develop a phobia of flying. People who have a specific phobia are aware that their level of fear and anxiety about the feared object or situation is unreasonable.

The most common subtypes of specific phobias are: animal, including animals and insects; natural environment, including bad weather, water, and heights; blood-injection-injury, including seeing blood from an injury, injection, or medical procedure; situational, including bridges, flying, using public transportation, and tunnels.

The most common situation that people fear most is actually public speaking. However a fear of public speaking is categorized under social phobia. This is because the primary feature of social phobia is a fear of being in a situation in which a person will be evaluated by others or somehow do something that will cause humiliation and/or embarrassment to oneself in public. Public speaking is more about the fear of being under public scrutiny, than fearing a specific situation based solely on irrational fears of that situation.

Specific phobias usually tend not to cause much disruption in a person's life. Most people are able to lead normal lives easily able to avoid whatever specific situation or object the person fears. For example, if a person has a phobia of snakes it is unlikely that being afraid of snakes will disrupt the person's life, unless the person is a forest ranger or works in the snake collection at a zoo. However, a specific phobia can become a problem for people who have to travel by plane regularly for business and have a fear of flying, or are afraid of elevators and have to use an elevator on a daily basis either for professional or personal reasons.

Fortunately, specific phobias are very treatable. The treatment of choice consists of cognitive behavioral interventions. Medication may be used in an adjunctive manner depending upon the severity of the phobia.

Psychotherapy As A Treatment

Psychotherapy is the treatment of choice for specific phobias. Cognitive behavioral treatment interventions including exposure, systematic desensitization, cognitive re-structuring, and relaxation techniques include the best approach to treat specific phobia.

Exposure therapy is the most effective therapy treatment technique for specific phobia. This intervention entails exposing the patient to the feared situations or objects for continuous periods of time. This way the patient is forced to confront his/her fears within the context of therapeutic management. The patient starts with situations that are the least anxiety provoking, such as seeing pictures of snakes, and works up through a hierarchy of gradually more difficult scenarios to most anxiety producing, such as holding a snake. The patient is taught a variety of relaxation techniques such as progressive muscle relaxation and deep breathing so that the patient can control anxiety levels during exposure to the feared object or situation.

Systematic desensitization is another widely used intervention for specific phobia. It involves having the patient imagine being exposed to the feared object or situation. Again, the patient begins with the least anxiety producing scenarios and works up to the most anxiety producing scenarios. The patient is encouraged to imagine very specific details associated with the feared object or situation such as smells, tastes, sounds, visual cues, and touch in order to make it as real as possible. Relaxation techniques are used to moderate anxiety levels. Studies have indicated that exposure to the feared scenarios in a person's imagination is an effective technique for conquering specific phobias.

Cognitive therapy is also helpful to people with specific phobia since their fears about a particular object or situation are based on irrational beliefs. Using cognitive therapy, the therapist helps the patient to identify what the irrational beliefs are that the person holds to be true about the feared object or situation. Then the therapist helps the patient replace the irrational beliefs with more realistic or adaptive beliefs about the feared object or place. Sometimes this may also require educating the patient with correct information about whatever it is the patient fears. For example, a person's phobia of flying may be fueled by not understanding how an airplane works and the extensive training that airline pilots have. By educating the patient with this information it can help the patient form more realistic beliefs that help reduce the patient's fear.

Medications As A Treatment

There are not currently any psychotropic medications used just to treat specific phobia. Medications should only be used as an adjunctive treatment approach if the person is experiencing moderate to severe anxiety or panic when in the presence of the feared object or situation. Another factor to consider is how often the person is confronted with the feared object or situation. For instance, if the person is phobic of elevators and must use an elevator every day for work then medication is more strongly indicated. Also, the use of medication will depend on whether or not the person is effectively able to reduce their anxiety with relaxation techniques.

If medication is indicated for a specific phobia than the anti-anxiety benzodiazepine agents such as Alprazolam (Xanax) or Clonazepam (Klonopin) would be the drug of choice. This is because they are short acting, which means they work quickly to relieve anxiety, so they do not have to build up in a person's body over time to be effective. Also, since they are short acting they leave a person's system quickly so that the person does not have to deal with ongoing negative side effects of being on a continuous medication.

It is important to use benzodiazepines carefully, however, because they are highly physically and psychologically addictive. They should not be prescribed to anyone who has any prior history of addictions and/or substance abuse. These medications need to be prescribed and used with caution.

CHAPTER THREE

FEAR IN THE BRAIN

Fear may be as old as life on Earth. It is a fundamental, deeply wired reaction, evolved over the history of biology, to protect organisms against perceived threat to their integrity or existence. Fear may be as simple as a cringe of an antenna in a snail that is touched, or as complex as existential anxiety in a human.

Whether we love or hate to experience fear, it's hard to deny that we certainly revere it – devoting an entire holiday to the celebration of fear.

Thinking about the circuitry of the brain and human psychology, some of the main chemicals that contribute to the "fight or flight" response are also involved in other positive emotional states, such as happiness and excitement. So, it makes sense that the high arousal state we experience during a scare may also be experienced in a more positive light. But what makes the difference between getting a "rush" and feeling completely terrorized?

We are psychiatrists who treat fear and study its neurobiology. Our studies and clinical interactions, as well as those of others, suggest that a major factor in how we experience fear has to do with the context. When our "thinking" brain gives feedback to our "emotional" brain and we perceive ourselves as being in a safe space, we can then quickly shift the way we experience that high arousal state, going from one of fear to one of enjoyment or excitement.

When you enter a haunted house during Halloween season, for example, anticipating a ghoul jumping out at you and knowing it isn't really a threat, you are able to quickly relabel the experience. In contrast, if you were walking in a dark alley at night and a stranger began chasing you, both your emotional and thinking areas of the brain would be in agreement that the situation is dangerous, and it's time to flee!

But how does your brain do this?

Fear reaction starts in the brain and spreads through the body to make adjustments for the best defense, or flight reaction. The fear response starts in a region of the brain called the amygdala. This almond-shaped set of nuclei in the temporal lobe of the brain is dedicated to detecting the emotional salience of the stimuli – how much something stands out to us.

For example, the amygdala activates whenever we see a human face with an emotion. This reaction is more pronounced with anger and fear. A threat stimulus, such as the sight of a predator, triggers a fear response in the amygdala, which activates areas involved in preparation for motor functions involved in fight or flight. It also triggers release of stress hormones and sympathetic nervous system.

This leads to bodily changes that prepare us to be more efficient in a danger: The brain becomes hyperalert, pupils dilate, the bronchi dilate and breathing accelerates. Heart rate and blood pressure rise. Blood flow and stream of glucose to the skeletal muscles increase. Organs not vital in survival such as the gastrointestinal system slow down.

A part of the brain called the hippocampus is closely connected with the amygdala. The hippocampus and prefrontal cortex help the brain interpret the perceived threat. They are involved in a higher-level processing of context, which helps a person know whether a perceived threat is real.

For instance, seeing a lion in the wild can trigger a strong fear reaction, but the response to a view of the same lion at a zoo is more of curiosity and thinking that the lion is cute. This is because the hippocampus and the frontal cortex process contextual information, and inhibitory pathways dampen the amygdala fear response and its downstream results. Basically, our "thinking" circuitry of brain reassures our "emotional" areas that we are, in fact, OK.

Similar to other animals, we very often learn fear

through personal experiences, such as being attacked by an aggressive dog, or observing other humans being attacked by an aggressive dog.

However, an evolutionarily unique and fascinating way of learning in humans is through instruction – we learn from the spoken words or written notes! If a sign says the dog is dangerous, proximity to the dog will trigger a fear response.

We learn safety in a similar fashion: experiencing a domesticated dog, observing other people safely interact with that dog or reading a sign that the dog is friendly.

Fear creates distraction, which can be a positive experience. When something scary happens, in that moment, we are on high alert and not preoccupied with other things that might be on our mind (getting in trouble at work, worrying about a big test the next day), which brings us to the here and now.

Furthermore, when we experience these frightening things with the people in our lives, we often find that emotions can be contagious in a positive way. We are social creatures, able to learn from one another. So, when you look over to your friend at the haunted house and she's quickly gone from screaming to laughing, socially you're able to pick up on her emotional state, which can positively influence your own.

While each of these factors - context, distraction, social learning - have potential to influence the way we experience fear, a common theme that connects all of them is our sense of control. When we are able to recognize what is and isn't a real threat, relabel an experience and enjoy the thrill of that moment, we are ultimately at a place where we feel in control. That perception of control is vital to how we experience and respond to fear. When we overcome the initial "fight or flight" rush, we are often left feeling satisfied, reassured of our safety and more confident in our ability to confront the things that initially scared us.

It is important to keep in mind that everyone is different, with a unique sense of what we find scary or enjoyable. This raises yet another question: While many can enjoy a good fright, why might others downright hate it?

Any imbalance between excitement caused by fear in the animal brain and the sense of control in the contextual human brain may cause too much, or not enough, excitement. If the individual perceives the experience as "too real," an extreme fear response can overcome the sense of control over the situation.

This may happen even in those who do love scary experiences: They may enjoy Freddy Krueger movies but be too terrified by "The Exorcist," as it feels too real, and fear response is not modulated by the cortical brain.

On the other hand, if the experience is not triggering enough to the emotional brain, or if is too unreal to the thinking cognitive brain, the experience can end up feeling boring. A biologist who cannot tune down her cognitive brain from analyzing all the bodily things that are realistically impossible in a zombie movie may not be able to enjoy "The Walking Dead" as much as another person.

So if the emotional brain is too terrified and the cognitive brain helpless, or if the emotional brain is bored and the cognitive brain is too suppressing, scary movies and experiences may not be as fun.

All fun aside, abnormal levels of fear and anxiety can lead to significant distress and dysfunction and limit a person's ability for success and joy of life. Nearly one in four people experiences a form of anxiety disorder during their lives, and nearly 8 percent experience post-traumatic stress disorder (PTSD).

Disorders of anxiety and fear include phobias, social phobia, generalized anxiety disorder, separation anxiety, PTSD and obsessive compulsive disorder. These conditions usually begin at a young age, and without appropriate treatment can become chronic and debilitating and affect a person's life trajectory. The good news is that we have effective treatments that work in a relatively short time period, in the form of psychotherapy and medications.

CHAPTER FOUR

SUREFIRE WAYS TO GET RID OF BAD HABITS

Success, happiness and good health often elude us not because we lack good habits but because we have bad habits. Sometimes they are habits like procrastination or mindless spending. But at other times they can be addictions like smoking and gambling.

Knowing how our bad habits negatively influence our lives is rarely enough to break them. For example, all smokers are aware of the health consequences of smoking. Diseased lungs are displayed prominently in every cigarette pack. There would be no smokers in the world today if that worked.

This fails to work because we don't do our bad habits for the reasons we should not do them. No smoker has ever smoked a cigarette to get cancer. Students don't procrastinate to fail. So in order to break our bad habits, we must first remove the reason why we do them. In other words, we need to eliminate the desire to do the habit.

Once the desire is gone, it takes no willpower to break

bad habits, just as it doesn't take willpower to not do things we have no desire to do. It doesn't take much effort to stop yourself from eating live frogs because you have no desire to do it. Breaking your bad habits can be just as effortless. You just need the right belief and the right system.

Our Habits Controls Us

From the outside, it would seem that our bad habits is a matter of choice. Smokers, for example, do make the choice of trying their first cigarette. But no smoker has ever made a decision that they will keep smoking for the rest of their lives. We often fall into the trap thinking we can stop whenever we want, only to realize that we no longer have any control. When we watch the first episode of a TV show, we end up binge watching multiple seasons at a stretch because we cannot stop ourselves. Every addict wishes inside that he had never started because life was fine before their addiction but now they are hooked and cannot enjoy life without satisfying their craving.

Researchers from National Institute on Alcohol Abuse and Alcoholism trained rats to press a lever to get a piece food. The researchers later electrified the floor so that when the rat walked to get the food, it received a shock. In a different experimental setting, the rat recognized the danger in the electric floor and would avoid it. But when the rat saw the lever, the habits took over and the rat would press the lever and go for the food and get electrocuted every time. The rat could not stop itself in spite of being aware of the danger because the habits were so strong.

Similarly, dieters find it hard to resist junk, smokers struggle to quit and students procrastinate on their assignments in spite of being aware of the consequences it has on their lives. Strong habits create an obsessive craving which makes our brain behave on autopilot even if there are strong disincentives like loss of job, health, reputation, family or home.

When We Use Willpower to Quit, We Fail

We usually try to break bad habits using willpower, which makes us feel we are making a sacrifice. A Harvard study showed the 12 month success rates of people who used the willpower method to quit smoking with no education or support was 6%.

When using willpower to quit, we find life extremely unpleasant and difficult and have to be cautious all the time to prevent relapse. This is because the desire to do the habit always remains inside us.

10 % of former smokers who abstained from smoking for ten years showed ongoing cravings even years later. 3 Mere abstinence does not mean we have broken our habit. It just means we don't allow ourselves to do our habit. A person who does not drink

alcohol but who is constantly thinking about alcohol is not a non-alcoholic but is an alcoholic who does not let himself drink.

We see the benefits of breaking our habits but also believe it provides us with something which we are now depriving ourselves of. This makes us miserable, vulnerable and increases desire that begins to obsess us. We try to overcome this by not thinking about our craving but that only makes us more obsessed.

Believing our problems can be easily solved by doing our bad habits we begin to question our decision to break our bad habits. Finally, we accept defeat and cave in. This minor relapse makes us feel bad and we indulge in the very same habit that made us feel bad, to feel better.

We fail to break our bad habits not because we lack willpower but because we don't eliminate desire. Without desire, willpower is not required to stop, just as it doesn't take willpower to not do the things we have no desire to do.

Why Does Our Brain Form Habits If They Are Bad?

Habits is a way for the brain to save effort by making rewarding behaviour automatic. Without habits, you will have to relearn how to brush your teeth every morning. Habits are useful but the problem is our brain cannot tell the difference between good and bad habits. Behavior that gives us short-term rewards often becomes habits, even if they cause long-term harm. Overeating, procrastinating and smoking becomes habit easily because the rewards are instant and the pain comes later. Developing the habit of exercising is harder because the reward comes later.

Schultz from the University of Cambridge, trained a monkey named Julio to pull a lever when a shape appeared on computer screen. Pulling the lever gave Julio a drop of blackberry juice which made the pleasure centres of his brain light up. When his brain started craving for the juice, Julio was glued to the monitor like a gambler in a slot machine. If the juice arrived late or diluted, this craving would turn into anger & depression.

Charles Duhigg's book, "The Power of Habit" focuses on the 3 components of a habit. The first component is the trigger, which tells the brain to start doing a particular behaviour (shapes in Julio's monitor). The second component is the behaviour that is done (Julio pulling the lever). The third part is the reward for doing the behaviour (Julio's blackberry juice). The habit is formed when the brain starts to crave for the reward as soon as the brain sees the trigger. There is nothing programmed in our brains that makes us want to overeat or smoke. But over time we slowly develop a neurological craving for these things.

Break The Habit By Seeing The Reward As An Illusion

The first step to breaking your bad habit is identifying the reward.

What do you really get doing your habit?

If the rewards you think your habits provided were actually real, then you can break your bad habits, simply by switching your existing habit with a healthier behavior that provided the same reward. For example, if you eat junk at work for distraction, then you can break your habit simply by replacing eating junk with a healthier distraction that does not add to your waistline. This is the premise of the book "The Power of Habit" and this works well for weaker habits. But try telling a smoker to resist his urge for smoking when he is bored by entertaining himself on YouTube. He won't be a successful non-smoker for very long. This is because most rewards of our habits are illusions.

We often rationalize why we do our bad habits but all the reasons we use to justify our behaviour are an illusion, excuses, fallacies or based on myth. For example, smokers believe they need cigarettes to relax, relieve stress, to concentrate or to relieve boredom. But cigarettes do not give them any of this. If it did, they should be a lot more relaxed, focused and less bored than non-smokers.

Most of us brainwash ourselves in a certain way that keeps us doing our bad habits. Only by identifying what we think is the reward can we address and remove the myths we have about the reward. When we begin to see through the illusory rewards, we eliminate desire by realizing that there is nothing to give up.

What We Give Up When We Break Bad Habits?

What are we giving up when we break our bad habits? Well, most of the time you are giving up absolutely nothing.

We don't do our bad habits for pleasure. We do it to feel normal. This feels like pleasure. A drug addict feels miserable, anxious, stressed and angry when he is deprived of his drug. When he shoots up his drug, he gets relief from all the negative symptoms. The subsequent dose partially relieves the symptoms but also ensures that the addict goes through withdrawal again. This keeps the addict stuck in the vicious habit loop. Normal people do not experience the symptoms of the drug addict. When we look at this it is obvious to us that the symptoms the drug addict experiences are caused by the drug, not removed by it. But we fail to have the same understanding when it comes to our bad habits.

Our bad habits cause symptoms of craving that normal people don't experience. We do our bad habits to partially relieve the symptoms but it only keeps us stuck in the vicious habit loop ensuring we experience the symptoms of craving again.

Unlike drug addiction which might require a visit to rehab, the craving caused by most bad habits including alcohol and smoking can be killed immediately when the belief system is changed. If you are not entirely convinced that there is nothing to give up, you need to examine the rewards of your bad habits and see them for what they really are. Otherwise, you will feel craving and will have to use willpower to prevent relapse.

The 4 Illusory Rewards

If you think your habit provides any of the following 4 rewards, you probably have an illusory reward:

1. Relieves stress

2. Relieves boredom

3. Improves concentration

4. Relieves anxiety and gives confidence

We will address the common myths people have about each of these rewards which will help dispel the illusion.

Reward 1 - Relief From Stress & Relaxation

For many, habits provide relaxation and relief from stress. We all have several things stressing us out. Not just big tragedies but relatively minor things like work deadlines. We do our bad habits to relieve this stress and the stress does seem to go away. But what has really happened?

Apart from the environmental stress, we experience additional stress because of the aggravation caused by craving. Bad habits relieve this portion of stress it created through craving. But our real-world stress like work deadlines continues to exist. When we do our habits we feel better able to cope with this stress because we temporarily don't have the additional stress caused by the craving to deal with.

A study has shown that we fall back into our habits when we are stressed because we feel less anxiety and more in control when we do our habits. People who have been sober for years relapse when a major life catastrophe happens like a death of a loved one or divorce. This is because of a failure to understand that alcohol does not relieve stress but only adds to the problem.

The habits that we fall back on during times of stress need not be bad. In a study, students who habitually ate a healthy breakfast continued to eat healthy during the stressful period of their exams. Whereas students who gained extra weight during their exams had a habit of eating unhealthy. Consciously engineering your habits is important so that your habits make you better and not worse during times of stress.

Reward 2 - Relief From Boredom

Some people do their habit because they are bored. Boredom is a frame of mind and not a physical condition that can be cured. Initially, we are bored. Now we are bored and engaged in self-destructive behaviour. Our bad habits do not cure boredom. It just creates a temporary distraction that allows us to forget that we are bored.

If our bad habits did relieve boredom, then why do we have to engage in it multiple times or do it for longer periods at a stretch?

Most bad habits rob us of our energy and make us more lethargic, putting us in a state of mind where we cannot do anything else. Instead of doing something when bored like how a normal person would, we lounge around, do our bad habit and feel more bored.

If you know someone who plays excessive video games or who spends hours in front of the TV, you will see they are not any less bored. They will be extremely tired and will feel like shit for wasting so much time.

Reward 3 - Helps Concentration & Removes Mental Block

If you think your bad habits removes mental blocks and improves concentration, then you are not alone. Some of the greatest artists of the world including Van Gogh and Beethoven were addicts. But curing addiction does not lower creativity because your genes do not change. It is just your craving that goes away. So what really happens?

A study done on 96 undergraduates showed a reduction in the student's ability to do tasks that required visuospatial memory, when they experienced craving for chocolate. In other words, craving negatively affected the student's ability to remember.

Our bad habits cause craving which creates a distraction that makes it difficult to concentrate. When we need to concentrate we do our habits to eliminate the distraction caused by our craving. We give credit to our bad habits for helping us concentrate when it was responsible for the distraction to begin with. People without bad habits will not have problems with concentration because they don't experience the craving.

Over time people who believe that their bad habits help them concentrate begin to believe that it removes mental blocks. After you do your bad habits, your block will still exist, but only now you will get the job done just like how anybody would have done it. But your bad habits get the credit for helping you get the work done.

Your bad habits provide no mental performance advantage and believing it does is based on fallacy and myth.

Reward 4 - Confidence & Anxiety Relief

We acknowledge the relief provided by our bad habit as it removes the small amount of emptiness and insecurity. But we don't acknowledge that this emptiness and insecurity are the symptoms of our bad habits in the first placek.

People who have had their bad habits for many decades have been in a perpetual state of anxiety and emptiness so their bad habits seem to be the only way to get confidence and a relief from this feeling. Our bad habits do not relieve the anxiety in our lives, it causes it. People without bad habits never feel this insecurity or anxiety, to begin with.

Freedom from the self-loathing and dependency is one of the biggest positive changes people see in their lives when they break their habits. They are more relaxed and confident after breaking their bad habits and are better able to deal with their anxieties if it is not gone altogether.

Relief From Craving is The Only Reward

Craving and withdrawal can make you insecure, irritable, anxious or agitated. Though there is no physical pain, it causes mental agony giving us a feeling that something is not right. For example, smokers believe that withdrawal is a physical trauma caused by not satisfying their craving. But eight hours after putting out the last cigarette, a smoker is 97% nicotine-free. This happens every night during sleep. Only during the day does he feel the need to smoke every hour to fix his craving. After three days of not smoking, a smoker is 100% nicotine-free. Yet smokers relapse because of craving after months of abstinence. The truth is withdrawal and craving is almost always psychological even for smokers & alcoholics.

We associate our bad habits with pleasure because we see them satisfy our craving, but don't see them causing it. Our craving is not cured by our bad habits but is caused by it.

We might have started doing our bad habits for many reasons, but the only reason why we keeping doing them is to feed the craving. Every time we do our habit, the craving is satisfied temporarily. This provides a temporary relief, putting us in a normal state of mind. But by doing our habit, we have set ourselves up to experience craving again in the future. The more we feed our craving, the more it takes to satisfy it. Smokers go from one cigarette to chain smoking fairly quickly.

What we really enjoy is not our bad habits but the feeling we get when our craving is satisfied. It is like putting on tight shoes just for the pleasure of taking them off. This is why by breaking bad habits, you are giving up nothing.

Hidden Drivers of Bad Habits

Alcoholics Anonymous (AA) have a concept called dry drunk, where alcoholics stop drinking but still remain angry, selfish and narcissistic. Our bad habits are often symptoms of some inner conflict. Things like anger, shame, loneliness, fear and hopelessness that makes people start doing their bad habits, needs to be addressed first. Until the flawed beliefs are fixed, we will always remain vulnerable to relapse. The habit of procrastination, for example, can be fixed only temporarily, if the underlying fear of failure is left unaddressed.

Bad habits are a way for our sub-conscious mind to avoid the real inner conflict that exists inside us. The inner conflict is either a bitter truth ("I am ashamed of my past") or a distorted assumption ("I screw up everything" or "I am better than everybody"). This inner conflict is never a mystery but we make it a mystery because acknowledging the truth is uncomfortable. It is easier to think we have no choice or control over our lives than it is to take responsibility for fixing it.

The best way to fix inner conflicts is through therapy which works by bringing our inner conflict to light causing them to vaporize like a vampire. The next best way is service. Helping others has helped AA members reduce their desire to drink. A study of 195 addicted adolescents showed that treatment showed substantial improvement when it was accompanied by service. 10 This works because love neutralizes shame and service to others reduce obsession and craving by eliminating the inner conflict. Helpfulness may not help break bad habits by itself, but it addresses the internal conflicts that create craving.

The System To Break Bad Habits

Now that we have addressed the core beliefs and issues that make us do our bad habits, let us look at the step by step system to break bad habits. With this system, you will be able to break any habit easily and effortlessly without using willpower.

Helping Others Break Bad Habits

Do not patronize the person you are trying to help, by telling them why their habits are bad. They already know this and don't do their bad habits for the reasons they shouldn't do it. They do their bad habits to feel normal.

Do not tell them breaking bad habits is easy as it will only irritate them. Give them the support and praise to keep them moving forward.

Do not force them to break their bad habits. Even if they try, they will use willpower to quit and end up failing. Tell them that people who succeeded in breaking their habits did not use willpower but instead addressed their flawed beliefs. Tell them how their bad habits only remove their need to do the habit which is perceived as pleasure by the brain. But in reality, their bad habit do not give them anything.

When they start believing that they can break their bad habits, their mind will begin to open up and that is when they are ready to read this book. Mention that there is no pressure to break their bad habits. If they want to continue to do their bad habits after reading this book, they can.

Where To Go From Here

The key to making it easy to break bad habits is to make your decision final and certain. Don't worry whether or not you have broken your bad habit. Know that you have. Do not ever doubt your decision. Celebrate it. Withdrawal is entirely psychological and if you are sulking, it only means you have not addressed your belief systems yet. Revisit Steps 2 to 4 in the system.

Don't make the mistake of procrastinating and not applying what you have learnt. You can wait for as long as you want to break your bad habits but the right time will never come and your habits are not going to be any easier to break tomorrow.

Some people think their bad habits has not caused any problem yet, so it is not a big deal if they don't break their habits now. The best time to fix the roof is when it is not raining. Don't wait for things to go wrong before you fix your bad habits. Break your bad habits now.

CHAPTER FIVE

STRONGER FOR THE EXPERIENCE

Many of us don't realize how much our past is dictating our current and future lives. We think that we're being cautious and smart, that we're using hard-earned information from what happened long ago to avoid the same mistakes now.

Little do we realize that holding onto past occurrences just makes them happen again and again. In this book, I'm going to talk about why we hold onto the past, how it messes with our lives now, and how to let it all go.

The ego is the part of your mind that stays focused on the past. It has a really potent message about the past that it feeds you all the time, and that message is: Watch out, it's going to happen again.

This is one of the sly tricks of the ego; this belief alone is enough to keep you stuck. And it works like a charm.

The fear that what happened in the past is going to happen again makes us so scared that it keeps us from enjoying what is actually happening now. Instead of being open to different experiences and outcomes, we are riddled with fear that we are going to get hurt again.

When our minds are focused on something then it becomes our experience; our expectations become our realities. The reason this is true is because we cannot separate ourselves from our perception. What we perceive is what is real to us. If your perception is stuck on repeat in the past, then your present is repeating in the past too.

It isn't until we actually let go of the past completely that we can really move on and have a new experience. And the way to do that is by surrendering your fears.

You have to become willing to create a different reality. Your life will not turn out differently unless you do something different. And luckily, you can.

Here's how to let go of past fears that are cursing you in the present:

1. Notice when your fear surfaces—the one that says, It's going to happen again.

If we are going to let go of fears we have to recognize them first. Just noticing goes a long way; it's called gaining consciousness.

When you start to feel yourself getting a little anxious or fearful, stop and take notice. Think to yourself, "Oh here it is, I'm starting to get freaked out."

This step helps you start to disengage from the fear as the ultimate reality. It helps you to realize that you are not your fear.

2. Call out the fear.

Get clear about what you are afraid of. What happened? What are you afraid of happening again?

Maybe the fear is that when you opened-up to another person, you felt rejected. Maybe the fear is when you got close to another person, you lost yourself.

Name it (I would even suggest writing it down). Again, knowing what the fear is is the only way you can let it go.

When fear flies under the radar, it has the power to plague us without us even knowing it. If we are constantly inundated with unconscious fears then we start to develop other symptoms--illnesses, physical symptoms, depression, anxiety and other ailments.

If something feels "off," don't be afraid to investigate what's going on. You gain freedom by looking your fears in the eye.

3. Become willing to let the past go through forgiveness.

It always comes back to forgiveness because forgiveness equals letting go.

The things we are holding onto from the past are the things that we have not fully forgiven. They come in the form of resentments, but also just flat-out fears.

The essence of forgiveness is: I know that what happened was a mistake. I know that it happened because we (I, the other person, or both of us) were acting out of fear. I am willing to feel peace about it and let it go.

Big words. So important.

Forgiveness is a life-changing practice. It is absolutely crucial in creating a new reality in your present and future. For a detailed guide on the how to forgive, check out Why Forgiveness Will Change Your Life.

4. Recognize that peace lives in you.

Really. It does.

Often we want the people around us to mold and change so we can feel better. But actually if we are scared of the past (OUR past) then it's our job to regain a sense of peace.

Ideally the people in our lives will support us when we're scared, but ultimately it's not their job to make everything better. Once we realize this, then we stop relying so heavily on others to feel safe.

Prayer and meditation are great tools to bring you back into the present. If you simply close your eyes, feel your breath, and listen to your heart, you can easily re-center and orient yourself back to now.

Fear is only activated when we are focused on the past or the future. Anytime you feel fear, if you can make your way back to now you will realize that you are actually safe and well.

The next time you feel fear coming on, implement all four of these steps. They will help you come back to who you really are, which is a peaceful, joyful, magnificent person.

Just remember, you are much more powerful than your fears; you don't have to keep living them over and over again. When you choose to have a different experience in life, that different experience will also choose you.

CHAPTER SIX

PRACTICING MINDFULNESS MEDIATION

To effectively manage stress and anxiety, you need to calm down your amygdala's fear and panic. A mindfulness mind-set and stress reduction techniques are the antidote to being swept away or immobilized by stress and anxiety. Practicing mindfulness for stress and anxiety is an open, compassionate attitude toward your inner experience that creates a healthy distance between you and your stressful thoughts and anxious feelings, giving you the space to choose how to respond to them.

With mindfulness practice for stress and anxiety, you learn how to sit peacefully with your thoughts and feelings in the present moment, creating an inner calm to help contain and reduce stress and anxiety.

If I had to pick just one tool for dealing with stress and anxiety, I'd choose mindfulness. The use of mindfulness is supported by a growing neuroscientific literature, demonstrating actual changes to neurons in the amygdala following mindfulness training. Mindfulness-based interventions have gained the

COGNITIVE BEHAVIORAL THERAPY MADE SIMPLE

attention of therapists, educators, coaches, and even politicians and business leaders. This brain skill can have far-reaching beneficial effects, not only transforming brain neurons but improving immunity, health, life, and relationship satisfaction. Mindfulness for anxiety and stress has the potential to make not only individuals but even businesses, institutions, and societies more stress-proof.

In this book, you'll learn about mindfulness, its history in ancient Buddhist philosophy, and the current use in the West of mindfulness exercises as a widely accepted and effective mind-body practice for anxiety and stress reduction. You'll learn the qualities of a mindful mind-set and how to train your mind to be more mindfulthrough mindfulness meditation practice and mind-set change. Read on, and learn why "The Mindful Revolution," as Time magazine dubbed it, is the key to managing your stress and anxiety!

The Roots of Mindfulness

Mindfulness is both a skill and an attitude toward living that originated thousands of years ago as part of Buddhist philosophy. According to the Buddha, mental suffering (or inner stress) occurs because we cling to positive experiences, not wanting them to end, and we strive to avoid pain, sadness, and other negative experiences. This effort to control our mental and bodily experiences is misguided and out of touch with the reality of living. We can never escape loss and suffering because these are natural parts of life. Our experiences are always changing. Living things wither and die, to be replaced by new living things. The forces of nature are beyond human control.

The Buddha believed that although pain is inevitable, suffering is not. Suffering results from our attempts to cling to pleasure and push away pain. Buddhist teaching describes suffering in terms of being shot by two arrows. The first arrow is the pain and stress that are an inevitable part of being human. These types of stressors, such as aging, illness, and death, are beyond our control. The second arrow is the one we use to shoot ourselves in the foot by reacting to the natural experience of human suffering (or stress) with aversion and protest. It's as if we've become phobic of our own emotions! When we begin to feel stressed, we create mental stories of worry and regret that compound our mental suffering. We get caught up in negative beliefs about ourselves, regrets about the past, or worries about the future, taking us out of the present moment. Or we try to push our feelings of stress and anxiety away through addictions and avoidance. These strategies just make things worse. As one of my wisest supervisors once said, "The cover-up is worse than the crime!" Practicing mindfulness for stress and anxiety returns us to the present moment.

The Buddha also believed that if we can understand the nature of suffering and learn to accept pain and loss with compassion (rather than running away from them), our mental suffering will lessen. We may not be able to get rid of the first arrow of inevitable pain and grief, but we can get rid of the second arrow of self-created mental and emotional suffering with mindfulness-based stress-reduction techniques. By looking at our own inner experiences with a curious, nonjudgmental, and welcoming attitude, we can learn to better tolerate negative states of mind (such as feeling stressed and anxious) and relate to these experiences in a more kind, accepting way. Using mindfulness for anxiety and stress, by calibrating us for momentary neutrality, creates space for such tolerance. Another truth about suffering that the Buddha understood is that our thoughts, feelings, and physical sensations, like all other aspects of life, are transient and constantly changing. When we directly face and accept negative experiences, they'll move through us, rather than getting stuck. The Buddha also believed that living a life of peace, self-discipline, service, and compassion would create an end to suffering on a higher level.

University of Massachusetts Medical School professor emeritus Jon Kabat-Zinn was the visionary who first introduced mindfulness practice for stress and anxiety to the Western medical establishment. He reframed the Buddhist concepts using scientific terminology, added some meditation exercises and yoga stretches, and developed an intensive eight-to-ten-week mindfulness-based stress reduction (MBSR) program that included forty minutes of mindfulness meditation practice each day as homework. He recruited into the program a group of chronic-pain patients who weren't responding to regular medical treatment. Incredibly, these participants reported less pain, improved mood, and better mental health from the beginning to end of the mindfulness-based program (Kabat-Zinn 1982; Kabat-Zinn, Lipworth, and Burney 1985), and in comparison to a group of patients receiving the clinic's normal care (Kabat-Zinn, Lipworth, and Burney 1985). And thus the Mindful Revolution was born.

Today, mindfulness-based interventions for pain, stress, depression, anxiety, cancer, addiction, and chronic illness are accepted worldwide. The credibility of mindfulness exercises as an intervention for anxiety and stress and stress-related illness has been enhanced by its strong neuroscientific base. University of Wisconsin professor of psychology and psychiatry Richie Davidson has been instrumental in demonstrating how mindfulness works in the brain and how mindfulness for stress can change brain structure and functioning to facilitate stress resilience and mental health.

Dr. Davidson's research team used brain imaging technology to study mindfulness meditation techniques in Buddhist monks and novice meditators (Davidson et al. 2003; Lutz et al. 2004). Their findings suggest that "contemplative practices" such as meditation and mindfulness can improve compassion, empathy, kindness, and attention in the brain. These studies powerfully demonstrate neuroplasticity—that even adult brains can change their structure and pathways with repeated practice of new habits. By practicing mindfulness techniques for stress, you can learn to redirect the emotional reactivity of your stress response into more calm, peaceful, and attentive states.

Mindfulness and Your Amygdala

Your feelings of stress and anxiety result from your amygdala's seeing external experiences or even your own emotions as threats. This is a problem, both because it's impossible to escape many stressful experiences and because it's impossible to stop stress-related emotions from arising.

The location of your amygdala—in the middle of your brain, beneath your cortex—means that it receives information about threats and initiates your stress response very rapidly, sometimes even before the thinking parts of your brain know what's happening. In other words, you can't stop your amygdala from trying to protect you by initiating a stress response when it senses a change in circumstances that could lead to danger, loss, or pain. And you probably wouldn't want it to! Without your amygdala, you might waltz into traffic, stick your hand on a hot stove, or hang out with unsavory characters without realizing the danger. But you do need to manage your amygdala so that it doesn't compound your stress and anxiety or create unnecessary suffering for you. Using mindfulness techniques for stress and anxiety allows your prefrontal cortex to calm your amygdala when it overreacts, so you can avoid the Buddha's second arrow (unnecessary suffering), resulting in stress reduction.

Mindfulness skills are the antidote to the amygdala's rapid reactivity. With mindfulness techniques for anxiety and stress, you can learn to slow things down long enough for the prefrontal cortex to get on board and steer you through the stressful rough waters. Mindfulness meditation practice also creates a calm, relaxed state of mind that prompts your parasympathetic nervous system to calm down the physiology of the "fight, flight, or freeze" response and return to balance. Mindful states of mind send signals to your body that slow down your breathing and your heart rate. They tell your parasympathetic nervous system that the danger has passed and it can bring the body back to balance. In the next section, you'll learn more about what mindfulness for stress and anxiety is and how you can practice mindfulness-based stress reduction to calm down your amygdala.

What Is Mindfulness?

Think of mindfulness for stress and anxiety as both an attitude toward living and a resilient brain skill that reduces your amygdala's reactivity. Jon Kabat-Zinn defined mindfulness practice as a way of paying attention purposefully and with nonjudgmental acceptance to your present-moment experience (1994). When you practice adopting the stance of mindfulness for anxiety and stress toward your own experience in the moment, whatever that may be, you open up the space to sit peacefully with and examine your thoughts, feelings, or body sensations, rather than following your amygdala's instructions to run away, be overwhelmed, or react impulsively. You replace fear of your own inner experience with a curious, gentle, welcoming attitude—free of judgment, self-blame, and aversion. Mindfulness techniques for anxiety and stress reduction allow you to remain grounded in the present moment even when you face difficult stressors, so that your stressful feelings and anxiety feel more manageable or less overwhelming.

Mindfulness for stress and anxiety is a state of mind, a deliberate, purposeful, focused way of looking at your experience in the present. Rather than experiencing stress or anxiety on automatic pilot, when you're mindful, you look at your feelings of stress and anxiety from an observer vantage point. With mindfulness practice, you're aware of the stress and anxiety flowing through your mind and body without feeling totally merged with it. You maintain the awareness that stress is a moving, dynamic state that's flowing through you but that it isn't all that you are. You're more than whatever's happening in your mind and body at the moment. Mindfulness meditation teachers often use the metaphor that you are the sky and your thoughts and feelings are clouds. The clouds float by, but the sky is always there. The sky provides the canvas for the clouds to float on. So you're the sky, and your feelings of stress and anxiety are the clouds. You can sit out the storm until the sky is clear!

The most common anchor used in teaching mindfulness techniques for stress and anxiety is your breath. When you get stressed or anxious, your breathing becomes faster and more shallow as your sympathetic nervous system readies your body for fighting or fleeing. When the stressful situation is over, your parasympathetic nervous system begins slowing your breath and heart rate to put the brakes on your stress response. With mindfulness exercises for anxiety and stress, you deliberately focus on your breath in a way that slows it down, even though this isn't the explicit goal—the goal is just to watch your breath. With mindfulness for anxiety and stress reduction, your breathing becomes slower and more rhythmic, which slows down your heart rate. The parts of your brain responsible for sensing movement and breathing send signals to your amygdala that the threat is over, and the whole system begins to calm down.

The best way to understand how your body reacts to mindfulness for stress and anxiety is to experience mindfulness-based stress reduction. The following mindfulness meditation technique will teach you to focus on your breath in a mindful way. The more often you do these sorts of mindfulness exercises for anxiety and stress, the more quickly you'll develop an attitude of mindfulness.

Exercise: A Simple Breath Awareness Meditation

Here are some instructions for a basic breath awareness mindfulness meditation. Do this once or twice a day for two weeks, and observe what happens. There's no right or wrong way to do this mindfulness practice for stress and anxiety. Try to accept whatever your individual experience is. The goal is not to achieve perfect focus on your breath, but rather to learn how your mind works! It's normal for your mind to wander, but when you catch your mind wandering and deliberately bring it back, you're learning to mindfully control the focus of your attention.

1. Pick a comfortable, quiet place where you won't be disturbed.

2. Sit with your spine upright on a cushion on the floor or a chair. If you use a chair, make sure your feet are touching the ground. Close your eyes, or maintain a soft, unfocused gaze.

3. Begin to notice your breathing. Try to maintain an open and curious attitude. Notice where your breath goes when it enters and leaves your body.

4. Don't try to force or change your breath in any way. It may change naturally as you observe it.

5. If your mind wanders, note what it's doing, and then gently bring your attention back to your breath.

6. Continue observing your breath for eight to ten minutes. At the end of the practice, notice how your mind and body feel, then slowly come back to the room.

As you continue this mindfulness practice for stress reduction for two weeks, notice if your mind resists the idea of change by creating judgmental thoughts such as I won't be able to keep it up or It won't do any good. You don't have to believe your judgmental thoughts; just notice them. Try to replace your judgmental attitude with one of curiosity, and keep an open mind so that you don't prematurely limit your experience.

In addition to paying attention in an open, nonjudgmental way, there are other characteristics of a mindful state of mind that create a powerful shift in brain functioning. In the next section, we'll discuss them in detail.

Characteristics of a Mindful State of Mind

Being mindful is more than meditating or focusing on your breath. Rather, it's a state of mind, characterized by the following attributes.

1. An Observing Stance

Mindfulness for anxiety and stress doesn't take away your stressful thoughts and feelings, but it changes your relationship to them. It's as if you're an observer who can look at these feelings without getting consumed by them or pushing them away. Thus, being mindful gives you more mental space and freedom. You don't have to be controlled by your stress response; you can redirect your focus, thereby gaining more control over your behavior when stressed.

2. Slowing Things Down

When your amygdala senses a stressor, it acts very quickly to "hijack" your brain for emergency action. However, not every stressor is an emergency, and successfully dealing with most stressors requires thinking of solutions, tolerating anxiety and uncertainty, and adapting to new situations. These are all functions of your prefrontal cortex, which is slower to receive and process information than your amygdala. Therefore, the first step in being mindful is to slow things down so that you can take a broader view of the situation before reacting.

Mindfulness for stress and anxiety moves your mind out of "acting" mode into "watching" mode, taking away the sense of urgency and giving your mind and body time to get back in sync.

3. Focusing on the Present Moment

When you practice mindfulness for anxiety and stress, you focus your attention deliberately and openly on what's happening in the present moment, both within you and around you. You may notice and describe your sensory experience—what you're seeing, hearing, feeling, or smelling right at that moment. Or you may focus on your breath to see what's happening inside and to ground yourself. This awareness of the present helps you stop ruminating about the past or worrying about the future.

4. Replacing Fear with Curiosity

Mindfulness for anxiety and stress replaces fear and emotional reactivity with an open, spacious curiosity. What's that thought or feeling that's arising? What does it look like and feel like? Is this something helpful or important that you want to focus on, or is it just an automatic event that you can observe as it passes through you? How does this emotion or experience change and unfold over time?

5. Openness and Non-judgment

Non-judgment is a key part of a mindfulness practice for stress and anxiety. When your amygdala triggers your stress response, you automatically begin to label the situation or your reactions as a threat that you need to escape. This is the aversion that the Buddha referred to as the second arrow. By observing your judging mind—a key mindfulness technique—you can avoid automatically buying into these negative judgments. You can then deliberately redirect your mind back to observing your thoughts and feelings with an open mind. This transforms your experience of stress by taking the terror and panic out of it.

6. An Attitude of Equanimity

Based on the Buddha's original teachings about non-attachment to pleasure or pain, a mindfulness attitude is one of peace, balance, and equanimity. To have equanimity means to let go of "needing" things to be a certain way. Equanimity keeps us from getting shot by that second arrow of addictive cravings or feelings of panic and desperation.

Everything is impermanent, everything is changing,

and many important life outcomes are at least partially out of our control. Therefore, we need to stand firm and not be swept off balance by stress and anxiety.

7. "Being" Instead of "Doing"

When you're stressed, your amygdala creates an impetus for action to eliminate the threat so that you can be safe. Finding solutions or learning new skills in a stressful situation requires a goal-oriented mind-set. But your mind and body also need periods of rest and quiet so that you don't get depleted by too much "doing." Mindfulness for stress and anxiety teaches you how to just "be" in the moment, without any particular goal or outcome and without judging your experience or wanting to be rid of it.

In the next section, you'll learn to deliberately focus on your body or your sensory experience with mindful openness and curiosity.

The "How" of Mindfulness

It sometimes takes weeks or even months of practice to really understand what it means to be mindful. Following are different ways of practicing mindfulness for stress and anxiety. Try all of them, or find the one that works best for you. Research shows that practicing mindfulness for at least thirty minutes per day can actually shrink your amygdala (Hölzel et al. 2011).

Optimize your environment for practicing mindfulness for anxiety and stress. You may want to create a "meditation corner" with a comfortable pillow and some pleasant objects for you to focus on. A scented candle, a flower, or a smooth stone can be an anchor for your mindful attention, as I'll describe later in the book. Set aside a time every day for mindfulness practice, and put it in your schedule. You can practice mindfulness for stress and anxiety lying in bed, sitting cross-legged or in a chair, or even while walking, as you'll see below. Find the way that works for you. You don't always have to practice for thirty minutes. Studies show that five to twenty minutes of meditation per day for five weeks creates some of the same brain changes as longer periods of meditation (Moyer et al. 2011) I suggest you start with eight to ten minutes a day of formal practice and then gradually increase the length of your mindfulness meditations.

And so your mindfulness journey for stress reduction begins.

Exercise: Mindfulness of Your Breath

This mindfulness practice is the one I use most frequently with my clients because it allows you to really feel and connect with your breath and also to feel grounded and solid in your body. It's my adaptation (with permission) of a mindfulness practice used by Daniel Siegel, author of many books and courses on mindfulness and the brain. This version of the instructions is for when you sit upright on the couch. Feel free to adapt the wording if you're lying on the floor or bed.

1. Sit comfortably on the couch with an upright yet relaxed pose.

Now close your eyes or maintain a soft gaze. Let your mind and body begin to settle into the practice, noticing what your body feels like.

2. Focus your attention on your feet. Notice all the parts of your feet that are touching the floor. Notice your toes; where your toes join your foot; the middle of your foot; your heel; your ankle; the whole bottom of your foot; the inside and the outside.

3. Let your feet sink into the floor, noticing the support of the earth and feeling it ground you.

4. Begin to notice all the parts of your body that touch the couch— the back of your thighs, your seat, perhaps your back, your arms, and your hands. Let your hands and feet sink into the support of the couch and floor. Notice how your body feels as you sit, supported by the couch and floor.

5. Begin to notice your breath. Just breathe easily for a few breaths, noticing where your breath goes as you breathe in and as you breathe out. Notice the pause

between your in-breath and your out-breath. If your mind wanders—as it probably will, because that's what minds do—just notice where it goes for an instant and then slowly, gently, direct your attention back to your breath.

Continue to do this as you begin to notice your breath in your nose, chest, and belly.

6. Slowly, bring your attention to your breath as it enters your nostrils. Notice whether it's hot or cold, light or heavy, and slow or fast. How does it feel? Notice where your breath touches your nostrils as you breathe in and as you breathe out. Continue to notice your breath in your nostrils for a few minutes.

7. Begin to notice your breath in your chest. Notice how your chest moves up and down with your breath like a wave, moving up as you breathe in and down as you breathe out. Just notice your chest as it expands and contracts with your breath. Watch the rhythmic wave in your chest as you breathe in and as you breathe out.

Continue watching your chest for a few minutes.

8. Direct your attention downward, toward your belly. You can put your hand on your belly to help you connect with the spot just below your belly button. This spot is at the very core and center of your body. Notice how your belly moves out when you breathe in

and how it moves in when you breathe out. There's no need to force or change your breath in any way. And if your mind wanders, bring it back to your belly kindly and gently. As you notice your breath in your belly, notice whether your breath changes or stays the same. Notice the rhythm of your breath in your belly.

9. As you notice your breath in your belly, begin to expand your attention outward toward your whole body. Begin to notice your whole body breathing as a single unit—breathing in and breathing out in a slow, steady rhythm. Notice the waves of breath as they move in and out of your body—filling your nose, the back of your throat, your chest, your ribcage, your belly, and your whole body with fresh, cleansing air. Notice how your breath travels through your body, and see whether it seems to open up any space in the area it touches. Just notice the rhythm of your whole body breathing as one: first the in-breath, then the pause between the breaths, and finally the out-breath. Breathing in and breathing out...

10. Slowly, begin to bring your attention back to the couch, to your hands and feet. Slowly open your eyes and begin to notice the room around you. Take your time, and notice how your body feels now. Is there any difference from when you began the mindfulness practice?

When my clients do this mindfulness practice, many

report a deep sense of peace, comfort, and calm. Feeling stressed can create tension, tightness, and constriction in your body, particularly in your chest and belly. This mindfulness-based stress-reduction practice can help open up space in these areas. A mindful focus creates distance from feelings of stress and generates a sense of peace and well-being.

Your breath is a powerful anchor for your attention, but this isn't the only way to practice mindfulness for anxiety and stress. You can also use your senses to create a sense of present-moment awareness and inner peace, as you'll see in the next mindfulness practice.

Exercise: Mindfulness of Your Senses

When your amygdala sounds the alarm bells, you lose touch with the present moment as your emergency response kicks in. You may feel compelled to "do something" about the stressor or to run away from the overwhelming feelings. By deliberately focusing attention on your senses instead, you move from a "doing," "getting," or "avoiding" mindset to "noticing and describing" what's around you. This mindfulness technique for stress reduction helps you feel more present and connected. We connect with the outside world through our senses. When we're mindful of what's around us, we gain awareness that we're part of a larger world of living and inanimate objects. Connecting with your senses can also be a way of what psychologist Rick Hanson (2009) calls taking in the good, or deliberately directing your brain to focus on relaxing or pleasant things in a way that helps calm down your stress response.

Walking in nature is a wonderful way to practice mindfulness of the senses. Being outdoors and close to nature has a calming influence on your brain and body, a natural backdrop for mindfulness meditation for anxiety. When you can't get outside, you can still practice mindfulness of your senses by adjusting the following practice to your situation. You can sit on your deck or in your garden or even look out the window, or you can look at pictures or photographs of nature scenes.

Exciting new research shows that walking outside in green spaces or even looking at nature scenes can increase your mind and body's resilience to stress. A study of college students (Bratman et al. 2015) showed that walking in green campus parkland reduced anxiety and worry more than walking in a busy street and had some cognitive benefits as well. In another study (Van den Berg et al. 2015), students were shown one of two types of pictures: either nature scenes, with trees and empty pathways, or urban scenes, with cars and people. They were then given a stressful math test. Those who had been shown pictures of trees had faster cardiovascular recovery (for example, their heart rate returned to normal more quickly after the test was over) than those who had viewed urban scenes. Measures of vagal tone showed that their parasympathetic nervous systems were better able to put the brakes on their "fight or flight" response. Benefits of mindfulness for stress reduction can occur whether the scene is one or three dimensional.

Mindfulness of Your Senses in Nature

As you walk or sit in nature, begin to notice your surroundings as a whole, noticing also how you feel in these surroundings. Notice that you're not alone— you're a part of the rhythm and pace of nature.

1. Bring your attention slowly to what you see. Notice the colors: the rich browns of the earth, the greens of the trees, or the blues of the sky or water. Are the colors bright or muted? Notice which ones draw your attention. Notice light and shadows, shapes and textures. Which surfaces are smooth, and which are uneven? Which are shiny, and which are dull? Which have sharp angles, and which are rounded? Just notice everything that you see. Now pay particular attention to one object—perhaps a tree or a flower— and notice its color, shape, and texture.

2. Focus on what you hear. Perhaps you hear the chirping of birds, the sound of the wind, or a babbling brook. Notice the sounds your feet make as they crunch on the gravel or sink into the earth. Do you

hear people's voices? Do you hear a dog barking? Notice the pitch and rhythm of the sounds. Which ones draw you in? Notice how the sounds emerge and then fade away—try to notice the silence between the sounds. Now pick one of these sounds to focus on. Notice its tone, pitch, and rhythm. Notice whether it stays the same or changes.

3. Notice what you smell. The smells around you may be sweet or spicy, earthy or fresh, faint or intense. Now pick just one smell to focus on—perhaps the breeze, the earth, or the flowers—and notice everything you can about it.

4. Notice what you feel. Notice the temperature of the air. Notice the feeling of the sun or the fresh breeze on your skin. Notice whether the air is moving fast or slow. Notice the feeling of the ground beneath your feet.

5. Notice how you feel inside your body. What's it like inside your chest, your back, and your belly? Do you feel any more spacious and calm than when you began this practice? Do you feel any part of you letting go of tension?

6. Notice how your feet feel as you walk. Try to slow the pace of your walking so that you notice each step: Right foot up, moving forward, and then down. Left foot up, moving forward, and then down…

For a short version of this mindfulness practice for stress reduction, pay attention to just one sense.

For example, focus only on what you see, hear, smell, or feel. Or just notice each step you take as you walk, without focusing on your surroundings. You can also do this mindfulness practice for stress and anxiety just about anywhere, at any time—not just in nature.

Exercise: Mindfulness of Objects

Another mindfulness exercise to calm your stressed-out brain is to focus on what's around you. If you're feeling stressed or anxious while making a presentation, interviewing for a job, taking an exam, or getting ready for an important dinner party, try silently naming three objects in the room and describing their color, shape, and texture as a quick and easy way of moving your mind from "fight, flight, or freeze" mode to "notice and describe" mode.

At home, create a "mindfulness corner" where you keep objects with interesting colors, textures, smells, or sounds. Use it as a sanctuary when you feel stressed, or simply practice your mindfulness exercises for anxiety and stress reduction there daily.

Each time you visit your "mindfulness corner," spend a few minutes examining the sensory qualities of each object. Look at it, touch it, smell it, and taste it if appropriate. Things that might work well for this purpose include seashells, smooth stones, scented candles, mints, sprigs of lavender or rosemary, flowers or leaves, lemons, small glass bottles, wooden beads, soft fabric, and hand cream. You can also buy traditional meditation objects such as a mindfulness bell, a Tibetan singing bowl, a small statue of the Buddha, or a Himalayan salt candle.

The options are limited only by your budget!

The exercises in this book are great ways to learn and practice mindfulness for anxiety and stress. Yet, as we discussed earlier, mindfulness is also a state of mind and a way of living that's larger than any particular practice.

Practicing mindfulness teaches you a stress-proof attitude that you can integrate into every aspect of your daily life. And the more you integrate mindfulness or stress and anxiety into your life, the more opportunity you'll have to calm your amygdala when it starts trying to hijack your brain. In the following section, you'll learn some ways of making mindfulness part of your daily routine.

Integrating Mindfulness into Your Everyday Life

When you're feeling stressed or anxious, it's often because you have too much to do and too little time or because you're dealing with an emotionally difficult situation. Stress takes your mind away from the present moment as your amygdala focuses your attention on what will happen if you don't solve the problems or complete the tasks. Your mind may get tired and murky; you may find yourself getting distracted or zoning out instead of focusing on what's most important. You may run around on automatic pilot as your heart races and your breathing shortens in "fight, flight, or freeze" mode. These triggers serve to remind you to choose mindfulness to deal with stress and anxiety.

The following practice is adapted from a practice used by Dr. Elisha Goldstein (Goldstein 2010). Use it to become more mindful from the moment you wake up until you go to bed at night, constantly redirecting your brain back to the present and weakening your amygdala's power to take away your sense of peace and connection with the world.

Integrating Mindfulness into Your Daily Routine

When you first wake up, instead of jumping out of bed, make time for the STOP practice described here. It'll help you start your day off on a mindful note. Continue to use this mindfulness practice throughout the day whenever you begin to feel stressed or anxious, as a way of grounding yourself when stress begins to creep in.

1. Stop. Stop whatever you're doing, and bring your mind back to the present moment.

2. Take a breath. Take a few deep breaths to slow down your "fight, flight, or freeze" response.

3. Observe. Begin to notice what you're feeling, thinking, and doing.

What's going on in your body? Describe any bodily sensations (such as tightness in your throat or shoulders) you become aware of. Is there an emotion word you can use to describe these feelings (such as "angry" or "scared")? Try to stay in the moment with these feelings and "breathe into them": imagine sending your breath into the areas that feel tight, constricted, or activated by these feelings.

4. Proceed. When you're feeling sufficiently present and aware, go about your business in a deliberate way. You may want to simply continue what you were doing, but with a more mindful demeanor.

Here are some other ways to integrate mindfulness for anxiety and stress into your life as you get ready for and go about your day:

When you observe your morning routine, notice if your mind is already at work or school, worrying or planning how to deal with your daily tasks and challenges. When you notice your amygdala hijacking your thoughts, bring your attention back to the present moment. If you're in the shower, notice the flow, temperature, and sound of the water, the bubbles, and the smell of the soap. When you drink your morning coffee, notice the smell of the coffee beans, the warmth of the cup, and the taste of the first sip. As you eat your breakfast, slow down and pay attention to the sight, smell, and taste of the food and how it feels to chew and swallow. Mornings offer multiple opportunities to practice your mindfulness-based stress reduction skills.

Mindfully greet the other members of your household or your pets. Slow down and focus on what they're saying and their nonverbal expressions. Focus on your feelings of love for them.

Take time to say good-bye as you leave the house.

On your way to your destination, notice what your mind is doing. Try leaving the house a little earlier so that you can walk or drive more slowly. Let the things you would normally see as interruptions or obstacles (such as red lights or delays) be reminders to practice mindfulness for anxiety and stress reduction. If you feel yourself getting angry or impatient with the traffic or long red lights, direct your attention to your breath or focus on the things you see around you—the cars, the people walking by, the trees, the sky, and so on.

As you walk into work or school, drop off your children, or go about your errands, check in with your body and notice any tension.

Bring yourself back to the present moment by slowing down and focusing on your breathing, what you see around you, or the feelings in your feet as you walk. Do the STOP practice if you begin to notice bodily tension or negative emotions arising.

Practice STOP before checking your phone, checking your e-mail, or logging into social media. Set time limits for these tasks, and don't let them sway you into mindless reactivity that distracts you from what's most important.

Use STOP or breath awareness mindfulness practices throughout the day.

Notice if your muscles are tense, if your breathing is shallow, or if your mind is wandering. Notice if you're feeling reactive, spaced out, or focused and alert. Change your focus by moving or stretching for a few minutes, practicing mindful breathing, or getting some fresh air.

Mindfulness is a skill you learn through repeated practice. It represents a shift in perspective away from constant focus on stressors and amygdala-driven reactivity. It allows your mind and body to rest peacefully and enjoy the moment despite the stress. Stress can be there, but it doesn't have to consume you and take you away from the people you love, getting your work done, looking after your health, and being present in your life. But mindfulness for anxiety and stress is more than a change in attitude.

With a regular mindfulness practice for anxiety and stress reduction and by adopting a mindful attitude toward living, you can actually change the structure of your brain, as you'll see in the next section.

How Mindfulness Calms Down Your Amygdala

Researchers have been studying the effects of mindfulness on the brain and body for more than twenty-five years using sophisticated technologies such as functional magnetic resonance imaging (fMRI) to scan the brain in real time. They have measured effects of mindfulness on depression, anxiety, physiological responses, blood pressure, and resistance to illness. There's now a wide body of evidence showing that mindfulness meditation works to reduce your body and brain's response to stress, taking away some of your amygdala's power to steer you off course.

Mindfulness-based interventions are associated with improved mood, reduced anxiety, better coping when stressed, enhanced emotion regulation, and less physiological reactivity (such as sweating and rapid heartbeat) in response to stressors. A meta-analysis that pooled the results of twenty mindfulness studies concluded that "the consistent and relatively strong level of effect sizes across very different types of sample indicates that mindfulness training might enhance general features of coping with distress and disability in everyday life, as well as under more extraordinary conditions of serious disorder or stress" (Grossman et al. 2003, 39). This meta-analysis showed that mindfulness training reduced disability and improved mood and quality of life in people dealing with a variety of physical illnesses (such as cancer, chronic pain, and heart disease) and mental health issues. Mindfulness interventions have also been shown to reliably reduce anxiety, depression, and stress in healthy people (Chiesa and Serretti 2009; Khoury et al. 2013).

Studies show that mindfulness training for stress can make the amygdala less reactive to stressors. A study by researchers at the University Hospital Zurich (Lutz et al. 2014) focused on whether mindfulness training for anxiety and stress reduction could affect the brain when subjects viewed pictures designed to trigger emotions. One group of subjects was given mindfulness training, and the other group (the control group) wasn't. Then both groups were shown pictures while their brains were scanned. Subjects were given clues that indicated whether the next picture would be positive, negative, neutral, or unknown (meaning there was a fifty-fifty chance it could be positive or negative). The subjects in the mindfulness group were instructed to use their mindfulness skills (for example, noticing their reactions without judgment) when the clue indicated that an unpleasant or unknown picture was coming. The brain scans showed that, compared to the control group, subjects in the mindfulness group had less activity in the amygdala and in brain regions involved in negative emotion when they anticipated seeing negative or unknown pictures.

Repeated practice of mindfulness for anxiety and stress over weeks or months may even change the structure of your amygdala. In a study by Harvard Medical School researchers (Hölzel et al. 2011), an eight-week mindfulness course led not only to reduced stress and anxiety but also to changes in the brain: the amount of nerve cells and neural connections shrank in the amygdala but increased in the hippocampus. Neither of these brain changes was found in the control group.

Scientists have pooled data from more than twenty studies (Fox et al. 2014) to show that mindfulness for stress and anxiety reduction affects at least eight different brain areas associated with self-regulation, memory, focus, motivation, compassion, and resilience. In particular, mindfulness can strengthen your hippocampus, an area that has many cortisol receptors and can be damaged by chronic stress. Your hippocampus can help you mentally process and file away stressful memories so that they're less likely to be triggered later. This suggests that mindfulness practices can make your brain more resilient to stress.

These research results are exciting, because they prove that you don't have to live in a monastery or on a mountaintop to calm your amygdala and strengthen your hippocampus with mindfulness-based stress reduction techniques.

Practicing mindfulness for stress over time makes your amygdala less reactive to negative events or uncertainty in your environment and helps your hippocampus process stressful events more effectively. In this chapter, you learned about mindfulness for anxiety and stress as both a practice and an approach to living that can help you better deal with stress.

Mindfulness meditation has its roots in ancient Buddhist philosophy, but it has been adapted for Western use. Being mindful means having an open, accepting, and compassionate attitude toward your own experience in the present moment, whatever that may be. It means allowing, rather than pushing away your inner experience; it means being in the moment, rather than constantly worrying or rushing around.

Mindfulness-based interventions have helped reduce people's feelings of stress, lower their blood pressure, and improve their resistance to illness. Mental health professionals use such mindfulness interventions to treat depression, anxiety, and substance abuse. Mindfulness has also been shown to shrink the amygdala (the brain's alarm center) and protect the hippocampus from being damaged by stress. The mindfulness exercises in this chapter can help you reduce your reactivity to stress and anxiety.

CHAPTER SEVEN

RECOVERY GUIDE TO ANXIETY DISORDERS

Getting rid of anxiety disorders isn't the same as taking out the trash. If you take your trash out to the curb, it's gone forever, and won't come back. But when you try to dispose of chronic anxiety, you often find that this task is more like the child's game, "Whack a Mole", than it's like taking out the trash. Each time you hit a mole, more moles pop up. Every effort that you make to fight against anxiety, invites more of it.

So you need to be able to work smart, not hard, to overcome anxiety disorders. This guide will help you do that.

The Anxiety Trick

The fears, phobias, and worry that you experience with chronic anxiety disorders often seem "irrational", and difficult to overcome. That's because there is a "Trick" to chronic anxiety problems. Have you ever wondered why fears and phobias seem like such difficult problems to solve? The reason is that chronic fears literally trick you into thinking and acting in ways that make the problem more chronic. You can't learn to float through anxiety disorders if you don't understand the Anxiety Trick.

The outcome of the Anxiety Trick is that people get fooled into trying to solve their anxiety problems with methods that can only make them worse. They get fooled into "putting out fires with gasoline".

The Key Fears of Anxiety Disorders

There are six principal anxiety disorders. The fears are different, but each one relies on the same Anxiety Trick, and draws upon the same kinds of anxiety symptoms.

And in each case, the person tries to extinguish the fears by responding in ways that actually make the problem worse and more chronic. Here are the key fears, and typical responses, of the six main anxiety disorders.

Panic Disorder and Agoraphobia

A person with Panic Disorder and Agoraphobia fears that a panic attack will disable him in some way - kill him, make him crazy, make him faint, and so on. In response, he often goes to great lengths to protect himself from a panic attack, by avoiding ordinary activities and locations; by carrying objects, like water bottles and cell phones, that he hopes will protect him; by trying to distract himself from the subject of panic; and numerous other strategies will ultimately make the problem more persistent and severe, rather than less.

The fear of driving is often a part of panic disorder.

If panic attacks and phobias are your principal anxiety concern, my Panic Attacks Workbook is a useful guide to recovery from these problems.

Social Anxiety Disorder (or Social Phobia)

A person with Social Phobia fears becoming so visibly and unreasonably afraid in front of other people that they will judge her as a weak, inadequate person, and no longer associate with her. In response, she often goes to great lengths to avoid social experiences, hoping that this avoidance will save her from embarrassment and public humiliation. However, her avoidance of social situations leads her to become more, rather than less, fearful of them, and also leads to social isolation.

The fear of public speaking, and the broader fear of stage fright are considered to be specific instances of Social Phobia.

Specific Phobia

A Specific Phobia is a pattern of excessive fear of some ordinary object, situation, or activity. A person with a fear of dogs, for instance, may fear that a dog will attack him; or he may be afraid that he will "lose his mind", or run into heavy traffic, on encountering a dog.

People with phobias usually try to avoid what they fear. Unfortunately, this often creates greater problems for them. Not only do they continue to fear the object, but the avoidance restricts their freedom to enjoy life as they would see fit.

A specific phobia is usually distinguished from Panic Disorder by its narrow focus. A person with a fear of flying who has no fear of other enclosed spaces would likely be considered to have a specific phobia. A person who fears airplanes, elevators, tunnels, and bridges is usually considered to have Panic Disorder or claustrophobia. However, the fear of public speaking is usually considered to be a part of Social Phobia.

A person with a Blood Phobia may fear a variety of situations, but they all involve the prospect of seeing blood. A person with a fear of vomiting (either fearing that they will vomit, or that that they'll see someone else vomit) would be considered to have Emetophobia. The official definitions of some of these disorders will change in 2013, so don't get preoccupied with the label.

Whether you have one or multiple phobias, these are very treatable conditions.

Obsessive Compulsive Disorder (OCD)

A person with Obsessive Compulsive Disorder experiences intrusive, unwelcome thoughts (called obsessions) which are so persistent and upsetting that he fears the thoughts might not stop.

In response, he tries to stop having those thoughts with a variety of efforts (called compulsions). Unfortunately, the compulsions usually become a severe, upsetting problem themselves.

For example, a man may have obsessive thoughts that he might pass swine flu on to his children, even though he doesn't have the flu himself, and wash his hands repetitively in an effort to get rid of that thought. Or a woman may have obsessive thoughts that she left the garage door open, and repeatedly check the garage all night in an effort to stop thinking that. Not only do these efforts fail to rid the person of the unwelcome thoughts, they become a new form of torment in that person's life.

Generalized Anxiety Disorder

A person with Generalized Anxiety Disorder worries repeatedly and continually about a wide variety of possible problems, and becomes so consumed by worry that she fears the worry will eventually kill her or drive her to a "nervous breakdown". In response, she often tries a wide variety of "thought control" methods she hopes will enable her to "stop thinking about it." Distraction is one such effort. Unfortunately, the effort to stop thinking about it actually makes the worrisome thoughts more persistent.

If persistent worry is a big part of your anxiety concerns, The Worry Trick is a useful guide to reducing the disruptive role worry plays in your life.

Post-Traumatic Stress Disorder (PTSD)

A person who has witnessed or experienced some dangerous or life threatening event (a shooting or a car crash) fears that the subsequent thoughts and powerful reminders of that event will lead to a loss of control or mental illness. The powerful symptoms of fear and upset a person experiences when recalling a terrible event are reactions to that event. However, the person gets tricked into responding to these reactions as if they were warnings of an upcoming danger, rather than reminders of a past one.

And Depression, too?

It's very common for people to experience depression

in response to the way anxiety disorders have disrupted their lives. Less frequently, sometimes people experienced a strong depression before the anxiety set in, and this is a different kind of problem. Either way, depressive symptoms need to be addressed in recovery, so it's useful t

Exposure Therapy for Fears and Phobias

Exposure Therapy has been shown to be the most effective anxiety treatment for people with many anxiety disorders. You might already know that it involves practicing with what you fear, in order to become less afraid. But how does it work?

Exposure Therapy helps you retrain your brain. It's not just about "getting used to" the fear. It's about retraining your brain to stop sending the fear signal when there isn't any danger.

People struggle against anxiety attacks and phobias because they recognize that their fears are exaggerated and illogical. They try hard to talk themselves out of the fear.

But that doesn't help. So they end up trying to avoid the fear, and that, unfortunately, just strengthens it.

Exposure Therapy will help you retrain your brain to let go of phobias, anxiety attacks, and other forms of anxiety disorders.

Let's see how Exposure Therapy works.

Fight or Flight

When your brain gets a signal of danger, it triggers an immediate response, the familiar Fight or Flight response. That's a good thing, because when we face danger, we need to react quickly and powerfully.

Humans evolved in a different world than the one we inhabit today. It was a world full of predators, without police or deadbolt locks. Our main job was to get enough to eat each day without becoming food for somebody else. We needed a good emergency alert system to keep us out of the jaws of predators.

If we had relied on the thinking, intellectual part of our brain, called the cerebral cortex, to keep us safe, we'd be extinct. It's too slow. It's good for writing a speech, and figuring out your income tax, but not for making snap decisions about danger.

The part of your brain that handles these Fight or Flight responses is very different from the part of the brain you're most familiar with.

The Amygdala

The Amygdala, a little almond shaped part of your brain, is what makes these Fight or Flight decisions. The Amygdala works quickly, without your conscious awareness, because speed is vital in protecting against threats. You only find out what the Amydgala did when you feel its effects in your body (all the familiar panic sensations) and in your behavior (duck, run, escape).

Whenever we make a decision, there are two possible kinds of errors. One is a false positive. If you decide there's a tiger hiding in the tall grass, when there isn't one, that's a false positive. When you make a false positive error, you get afraid in the absence of danger, but you don't get eaten.

The second type is a false negative. If you decide there's no tiger hiding in the tall grass when there really is one, that's a false negative. When you make this false negative error, you feel okay, but you're gonna get eaten.

Your Amygdala doesn't care how many times it scares you unnecessarily. It just aims to keep you alive. It doesn't want to make any false negative mistakes.

If you experience phobias and anxiety attacks, and want to overcome them, you need a form of anxiety treatment which will retrain this part of your brain. The most direct and systematic way to do that is Exposure Therapy.

How Your Amygdala Works

Your Amygdala is always watching, passively, in the background, for some sign of danger. When it sees one, true or false, it presses the "fight or flight" button and fills you with fear. When the danger is real, that's a good thing. But your Amygdala works like it's still 27,000 B.C., and will often make the mistake of seeing danger when there's none.

It Learns by Association, not Reason or Logic

When you run away from whatever the apparent danger is, the Amygdala stands down and goes back to quietly watching. If you ran away from a mugger, that's a good thing. But if you ran away from a grocery store, or a dog on a leash, that's a bad thing. Now your Amygdala will be conditioned to see the grocery store or the dog as dangerous, and will make you afraid next time you see one.

The Amygdala learns by association. It associates the crowded store, or the dog, with danger. It doesn't learn by conscious thought. This is why you can't simply talk yourself out of a phobia or anxiety attack. The fear memory is stored as a conditioned fear, and can only be relieved by more conditioning, not discussion or reason.

It only Learns When You're Afraid

The Amygdala only learns when it's fully activated, when it spots something it considers dangerous. It only forms new memories and associations, new lessons, when you've become afraid. The rest of the time it's on autopilot, passively watching.

Do you see what this means? If you stay away from what you fear, your Amygdala will keep on "believing" the same old mistakes, without a chance to learn anything new.

How Can You "Talk" to Your Amygdala?

Your Amygdala only learns from experience. If you flee the scene every time you have an anxiety attack, your Amygdala learns that you should leave to be safe.

How can you get your Amygdala to learn something new? You have to activate it by exposing yourself to a trigger that gets you afraid. If you have a dog phobia, that would be a dog. If you have anxiety attacks on subways (or highways), you need a subway (or a highway). And you need to stay there with that fear until it gets a lot lower.

That gives your Amygdala the chance to learn that it got all worked up about nothing. That way, it can learn that dogs (or highways) aren't the threat that it had been conditioned to believe. And, with repetition, it will develop a new memory, one that lets you get on with your life without being disrupted by phobias and anxiety attacks.

Retraining Your Amygdala

That's how Exposure Therapy works. Exposure Therapy retrains your Amygdala.

You don't have to do this radically and quickly. What you need to do is to continually arrange to activate your Amygdala by exposing yourself to what you fear, and then stay in place, making sure that the fear leaves before you do. You can use a variety of coping steps to help you do that, or you can just "float", as Claire Weekes called it, and wait for the fear to subside. Either way, Exposure Therapy will enable you to retrain your Amygdala with new learning in ways it can absorb.

List of Tips

Tip One: Panic attacks: 13 tips to stop anxiety in its tracks

One in 10 people are believed to suffer from occasional panic attacks, often triggered by stressful events, while two in 100 UK people have panic disorder (recurring and regular panic attacks).

A panic attack is an episode of intense subjective fear, usually accompanied by symptoms such as trembling, sweating, heart palpitations and hyperventilating. So what can you do if you feel your panic rising?

Stand up tall

As soon as you feel a panic attack coming on, straighten your spine and stand or sit up straight. 'Not only does this trick you into feeling more powerful and in control, but it will also give you physically more space to breathe,' says Niels Eek , psychologist at personal development and mental wellbeing app Remente.

Get moving

Panic attacks can make our entire body seize up, responding to our perceived threat of danger. 'The best and most counter-intuitive thing to do is to start moving around,'. 'Do some stretches, go out for a walk, or simply walk around slowly.' Moving and exercise are found to instantly counter the effects of panic by reducing cortisol levels as well as lowering the risk of anxiety in the future.

Fiddle and fidget!

If movement isn't an option, for example if you are on a plane during take-off, try to distract yourself with a stress ball, some beads or even gum. 'Researchers at Tokyo Medical and Dental University found that repetitive and tactile motions distract the mind from the immediate feelings of panic'.

Splash yourself with water

Researchers in Japan found that cold water stimulates the parasympathetic system, which in turn slows down our heart rate, providing a calming effect. 'While you might finding the task of drinking water while you are panicking physically impossible, try splashing some on your face,' suggests Niels Eek.

Chew gum

A mental health study found that chewing gum for 14 days may improve levels of anxiety and mood. Chewing is known to reduce levels of the stress hormone cortisol found in the saliva. Fast chewing has been shown to have a more anxiety-busting effect than slow chewing.

Boost your magnesium

A study in the journal Neuropharmacology, found that low magnesium can make you anxious. 'Magnesium is the most important mineral for 'relaxing' nerves and muscles and is essential for the normal functioning of the nervous system, so is effective for panic attacks,' says nutritionist Shona Wilkinson.

Name your feelings one by one

Whenever you are in the middle of a panic attack, your brain struggles to focus on anything that isn't the immediate panic. 'However, if you start naming each feeling you experience, such as 'it's difficult to breathe' or 'I want to cry when this happens', it can help re-focus your brain and move away from the panic.

Try colouring in

Research has shown that focusing on a calming activity such as colouring in mandalas can help people with anxiety. It works by calming down the amygdala, the part of the brain that controls our fight or flight response and keeps some people in a state of worry, panic and hypervigilance, so if you feel the panic start to rise, start colouring. Findings from the study suggest that colouring in a reasonably complex geometric pattern may induce a calming meditative state.

Go herbal

Herbal remedies have proven to be beneficial in halting panic attacks. 'Herbs which may be helpful in reducing anxiety include Valerian, Passionflower and St John's Wort,' says nutritionist Shona Wilkinson. 'These herbs may be a non-drug way to help reduce anxiety and help bring about a more calm state of being.'

Carry medication with you

'Some people find that carrying some beta-blocker tablets with them can be helpful (these are nonaddictive tablets which could be prescribed by a GP or psychiatrist), and they work to switch off the bodily feelings of anxiety, such as heart palpitations and tremors,' says Psychiatrist Dr Ian Drever. 'Often just by having these tablets with them, it's reassuring enough to stop many people having a panic attack in the first place.'

Remember panic passes

Dr Drever urges you to remember that no matter how bad a panic attack feels, it can never hurt you. 'It may feel like you're going to stop breathing, suffocate or have a heart attack, but these are all features of a rush of adrenaline, and they will fade away with time, leaving no lasting trace. Panic always passes.'

Create a soothing playlist

Listening to music can help to reduce stress levels and quash anxiety. Classical music is particularly effective at slowing pulse and heart rate, lower blood pressure and decreasing levels of stress hormones. But it doesn't have to be classical – some people find that creating a playlist of music around 60-80bpm can be a really effective panic-buster.

'This makes intuitive sense as this is the speed of a resting heartbeat. It also helps to provide an external focus rather than on an excessive internal focus on what the body is doing in the heat of an anxious moment,' says Dr Drever.

Bring on your panic symptoms

The majority of panic attacks are accompanied by physical symptoms, such as an increased heart rate, inability to breathe, dizziness and others. 'Focusing on the symptoms and letting them take over can often make you feel worse,' says Eek. 'Instead, try inducing the symptoms on their own, outside of the panic attack – you will find that you have no fear of them and that your mind will eventually get bored and move onto other things.'

These tips are something you can definitely try, but if you're having serious panic attacks then it's important to see a GP and/or a CBT-psychologist. Treatments for panic attacks are really efficient, and if the above tips aren't enough, can provide a real, working solution.

Tip Two: Quick ways to calm your nerves

It is tough to control psychological strain; stress is a natural response to tricky situations and the outside world. Some circumstances are simply beyond our control, making coping hard to do. Fortunately, you do have control over how you react to situations. Learning healthy responses to stressors is a great place to start. As compiled from calmclinic.com, Oprah, Prevention and Women's Health magazine, here's how you can regain your cool even quicker than you lost it.

Chew a stick of gum

Researchers from Australia and England found that in moments of stress and anxiety, gum chewers felt less anxious and had 18 per cent less of the stress hormone cortisol in their saliva. "Chewing increases blood flow to the brain, which may make us feel more alert, and it may also distract us from stressors," says study co-author Dr Andrew Scholey, director of the Centre for Human Psychopharmacology at Swinburne University. The study suggests that chewing gum can de-stress you in as little as 10 minutes.

Brew black tea

The study of black tea —instead of green or herbal varieties — found it helps cut levels of the stress hormone cortisol circulating in the blood stream. People who drank four servings of black tea a day for six weeks were able to de-stress faster and had lower levels of cortisol after a stressful event, according to a study from University College London. Chemical compounds in the antioxidant-packed beverage may relax us through their effect on neurotransmitters in the brain.

Try a tennis ball massage

The International Journal of Neuroscience reported that a 15-minute self massage twice weekly can lower stress by soothing the sympathetic nervous system. It is an effective alternative, as compared to popping beta blockers and anti-anxiety meds. "Simply rolling a tennis ball over tense muscles like the spine, thighs and foot with the palm of your hand can trigger a calming response," says Dr Tiffany Field, director of Touch Research Institute at the University of Miami, School of Medicine.

Put pen to paper

A 2010 study in Anxiety, Stress & Coping found that writing about a stressful event for just 20 minutes on two different days lowered levels of perceived stress. Putting feelings on paper appears to organise thoughts and helps process unpleasant experiences and release negative emotions. This is a good way to confront your emotions, especially if you're naturally inclined to write. If things become jumbled, just keep writing. It's the process of thinking and recording your conflicts that is most important.

Tune in to music

"The body's internal rhythms entrain to the external rhythms of music, like when you go to the sea, and you start breathing slower and your heart rate slows down and starts moving closer to the rhythm and pace of the ocean. It's the same with music," says Dr Frank Lipman, founder and director of Eleven-Eleven Wellness Centre. A study in the Journal of Advanced Nursing found that patients who listened to songs of their choice were less anxious and stressed. Boost your mood with clocking in at least 15 minutes of tune time daily.

Take a tech break

Before technology and smartphones, when you left your home or place of work, you most likely turned off the thoughts and emails related to it, too. Research shows we need mental breaks to refresh our minds and shut off the continuous stressors of work or classes. In a study by University of California, Irvine, and US Army researchers, heart rate monitors showed that checking e-mails and attending work calls put subjects on constant high alert with heart rates that indicated stress. "We found that shutting off e-mail eases anxiety," says study co-author Dr Gloria Mark. Commit to no e-mail or social media activity for 45 minutes a day to begin weaning yourself off.

Start Counting Everything

The next time you feel panic setting in, start counting your sensations. As Anna Borges suggested on BuzzFeed, "Count five things you can see, four you can touch, three you can hear, two you can smell, and one you can taste." This is another distraction technique that requires you to focus in on things that are real — like the sounds in the room, or the feeling of your shirt against your skin — instead of just the panic in your mind. It's also a good trick to use when you're cooped up on a plane, or stuck some place where skipping around and dancing might attract undue attention.

Clean the house

Housework's repetitive nature can help release tension and calm anxious nerves. "We get lost in the rhythm of folding clothes, mopping or vacuuming, which can disrupt stressful thought patterns and trigger the body's relaxation response," says Dr Herbert Benson, director emeritus of the Benson-Henry Institute for Mind Body Medicine at Massachusetts General Hospital. Studies have found that cleaning carries emotional benefits — catharsis, clarity, control and change. These good feelings lead directly to self-improvement and empowerment. Who thought doing the dishes could have benefits!

Just Kick Back & Accept It

Sometimes none of the above techniques work and you find yourself fruitlessly naming feelings, or pawing at a wad of Silly Putty. When that happens, all you can do is accept that the next ten minutes are going to be kind of sucky, and simply let the anxiety wash over you.

And often, that's really the best thing you can do. According to Gummer, "One of the most powerful things that you can do in the midst of a panic attack is to accept it ... Accept that it's there. Feel it completely ... Yes, it can get pretty nasty. But usually at the point when I feel like my whole being is going to explode from so much anxiety, something almost unimaginable happens: a release." That's because panic doesn't last long. It's important to remember that it'll be over soon, and that you will survive.

While panic attacks feel pretty awful, they aren't actually life threatening. So the next time you feel one coming on, try your hardest to channel the nervous energy elsewhere. In the best case scenario, you'll stop the panic in its tracks. In the worst case, you'll spend some time distracting yourself (and dancing around) until the panic fizzles out on its own. Either way, it will end, and you'll be able to go on with your day. I promise.

Tip Three: Anxiety Scams on the Internet

Anxiety scams abound on the Internet, with promises of quick cures for panic attacks, phobias, and other anxiety problems. When you feel desperate, when your daily life has been so disrupted by chronic anxiety that you're ready to try anything, it's very tempting to log on and buy the next product you see.

Maybe it will help. But there's a good chance that you won't get the promised results. The worse result then isn't even the money you spent, it's that you become less hopeful about ever solving the problem. So it's important to choose your self help tools carefully, and not just grab the first promise you see. Claire Weekes offered hope and help. All too often, anxiety scams offer hustle and hype. How can you tell the difference? How can you be an informed consumer of anxiety products? Most importantly, how can you find something that works?

Here are some tips;

Beware of quick, easy "cures"

Anxiety scams promise quick, easy results. They claim that the great majority of people who use it are "cured" of their anxiety. They suggest that the creators of the product have some special secret or insight which contains great power to help you, something that no one else has thought of. They often offer statistics which can't be verified, and testimonials from people who can't be located.

Anxiety disorders are solvable problems, and most people who struggle with them can overcome them. But recovery does take some work. If the promise sounds too good to be true, it's probably an anxiety scam.

Look for people with professional credentials

The Internet is full of programs created by people with no professional training in health care, psychology, or any relevant field. They're generally people whose skills are in marketing and advertising.

They often try to turn this to their advantage by pointing out that many physicians and therapists don't know very much about anxiety disorders. This is unfortunately true, but it doesn't mean that the answer is to turn to Internet marketers. The answer is to find better sources of professionally trained help, and materials written by people with the training and background to be helpful to you.

Be wary of affiliate programs

On the Internet, anxiety scams are usually marketed and sold through "affiliate programs". In an affiliate program, people with products to sell offer others the chance to sell the product through their own web site and keep a commission, typically 50-75% of the sale price.

It's quick, easy, and cheap to set up, and affiliates can make some money with little effort. Nobody has anything to lose...except the buyers. This is why you'll see hundreds of web sites for these products.

This marketing has become so organized that there's even a market for buying and selling the articles that affiliates use to promote these products. Affiliates themselves often don't know much about the product, and pay free lance writers to do the writing for them.

Check out these examples. Here's an ad seeking 9 articles on "fat loss, dog training, and anxiety attacks". How about this one - 25 articles needed, for which the buyer will pay $1.50 each, on the topics of "hemorrhoid care, learn spanish quick, and cures for panic attacks".

Everybody needs to make a living, but this isn't how I want to get my health care problems solved!

How can you tell if you're looking at a product sold by affiliates? Just google the name of the product. If google returns lots of web sites advertising the product, all fairly similar, and linking you back to the same site for purchase, that's an affiliate program you found.

Compare prices

Most of the best self-help books for anxiety disorders sell for less than $20. Anxiety products on the Internet are typically priced far higher than that, even though they're often only digital files which cost nothing to reproduce. These products usually range in cost from $60 to $100. The prices vary because they often offer a "special low price that expires today!"

You can buy a small shelf of books by Claire Weekes for less than what you would pay for one anxiety scam. Dr. Reid Wilson, Dr. David Burns, and Dr. Edmund Bourne all have written excellent self-help books which sell for less than $20.

When the price seems really inflated, odds are it's an anxiety scam.

Seek information, not just advertising

A good self-help site will freely offer actual information that you can use. It probably has products for sale as well, but that isn't its only purpose. It will offer actual self-help information about anxiety disorders, and give you a clear idea of how the products can help you. The typical anxiety scam web site consists of screen after screen of high pressure reasons to buy, and lots of extras if you buy NOW. However, they rarely describe how their product actually works, or give you anything you can use. They just urge you to buy.

If you read through an entire web site and still can't tell what method the author proposes for you to use, odds are you're looking at an anxiety scam.

See if it's available elsewhere

The Internet is a wonderful medium. But why aren't these products also sold in stores, and large outlets like amazon? It's often because the product isn't good enough to get approval from third parties like editors, publishers, and retail distributors.

If these products were sold in stores, they'd attract a

lot more scrutiny. Reviews would appear in newspapers and magazines. Customers would thumb through the books on shelves. Some Internet marketers don't want this kind of attention. Their strategy relies on catching you when you feel needy - maybe when you can't sleep and you're desperately surfing the Internet for help - and get you to make that impulse buy when you're least prepared to make a careful, considered choice.

When you can only get it from one supplier, the odds go up that it's an anxiety scam.

I have so much trouble - isn't it worth a try?

It might be. These products are generally overpriced and over promised, but that doesn't mean there's never anything of value. You might get something out of it, even if it's only a placebo.

But it's not a good place to start. A better way to start might be to go to amazon.com and search for books about the problem you face. Read about the authors, read the reviews, and you can often read a sample of the work itself. The odds of getting useful help from books you find that way are much, much higher than just googling the topic.

If you do want to try out an Internet product, then investigate it as best you can, and take two more simple steps.

Don't buy groceries when you're hungry

If you've ever struggled to control your diet and your weight, you probably have heard this suggestion. Don't go to the grocery store when you're hungry and grab whatever appeals to you. Instead, make a shopping list when you're not hungry, and follow that plan when you go to the store. That way, you can shop in an organized manner, rather than impulsively.

Tip Four: The Anxiety Trick

The Anxiety Trick is behind most of the trouble people have with chronic anxiety. Have you struggled to overcome an anxiety disorder, only to get disappointing results, or even feel worse over time? You're being fooled by the Anxiety Trick.

This is a terribly common occurrence, and people mistakenly blame themselves for it. Here's a more accurate, and helpful, way to understand this common and frustrating problem.

What is an anxiety disorder? It's you getting tricked into feeling powerful fear in the absence of any danger.

It's because there's no danger that people seek help for these fears. People recognize that they're getting afraid when they're not in danger. If they were actually in danger, they would just protect themselves as best they could, and be better off for it.

With an anxiety disorder, people get afraid when they're not in danger. Their struggle to protect themselves from fear leads them down a path of increasing trouble. That's the anxiety trick.

How does this happen, that you feel fear in the absence of danger? This is the Anxiety Trick at work.

How You Get Tricked

* If you have Panic Disorder or Agoraphobia, you keep getting tricked into believing that you're about to die, go crazy, or lose control of yourself.

* If you have Social Phobia,you keep getting tricked into into believing that you're about to look so unreasonably nervous in front of people that you will be completely humiliated and be cast aside by your community.

* If you have a Specific Phobia, you keep getting tricked into believing that you're likely to be overcome by some external object (like an elevator) or animal, or by your fear of it.

* If you have OCD, you keep getting tricked into believing that you've set in motion a terrible calamity. You might fear that your neighborhood will burn because you left the stove on, or that your family will get poisoned because you mishandled the insecticide.

* If you have Generalized Anxiety Disorder, you keep getting tricked into believing that you're about to be driven mad by constant worrying.

In each case, the episode of fear passes without the expected catastrophe. You're none the worse for wear, except that you're more worried about the next episode. The details seem different, but it's the same anxiety trick.

What is the Anxiety Trick?

The Anxiety Trick is this: You experience Discomfort, and get fooled into treating it like Danger.

What do we do when we're in danger? We only have three things: Fight, Flight, and Freeze. If it looks weaker than me, I'll fight it. If it looks stronger than me, but slower, I'll run away. And if it looks stronger and faster than me, I'll freeze and hope it doesn't see so good. That's all we have for danger.

When people experience the fear of a panic attack, or a phobic encounter, or an obsessive thought, they instinctively treat it as a danger. They try to protect themselves, with some variation of Fight, Flight, or Freeze.

How People Get Tricked

People's natural instincts to protect themselves are what lead them to get tricked. See if you recognize your responses in these examples below.

A person with Panic Disorder gets tricked into holding her breath and fleeing the store (highway, theater, or other locale), rather than shifting to Belly Breathing. and staying there until the feelings pass.

A person with Generalized Anxiety Disorder gets tricked into trying to stop the unwanted "what if?" thoughts, rather than accepting them and taking care of present business as thoughts come and go.

A person with Social Phobia gets tricked into avoiding the party, or hiding in the corner if he attends, rather than say hello to a stranger and see what happens.

A person with OCD gets tricked into repeatedly washing his hands, or returning home to check the stove, rather than accepting the intrusive thoughts of contamination and fire and returning his energies to the present activities at hand.

A person with a dog phobia gets tricked into avoiding the feelings by avoiding all dogs, rather than spending time with a dog until the feelings pass.

What Maintains the Anxiety Trick?

You might wonder, why don't people come to see this pattern, of repeated episodes of fear which don't lead to the feared outcome, and gradually lose their fear?

The answer is this. They took these protective steps, and there was no catastrophe. They tend to believe that these steps "saved" them from a catastrophe. This thought makes them worry more about "the next time". It convinces them that they are terribly vulnerable and must constantly protect themselves.

The actual reason they didn't experience a catastrophe is that such catastrophes are typically not part of a fear or phobia. These are anxiety disorders, not catastrophe disorders. People get through the experience because the experience isn't actually dangerous. But it's understandably hard for people to recognize that at the time. They're more likely to think they just had a "narrow escape". This leads them to redouble their protective steps.

It's the protective steps which actually maintain and strengthen the Anxiety Trick. If you think you just narrowly escaped a catastrophe because you had your cellular phone, or a water bottle; or because you went back and checked the stove seven times; or because you plugged in your iPod and distracted yourself with some music, then you're going to continue to feel vulnerable. And you're going to get more stuck in the habit of "protecting" yourself by these means.

This is how the problem gets embedded in your life. You think you're helping yourself, but you've actually been tricked into making it worse. That's how sneaky this Trick is.

This is why my patients so often say, "the harder I try, the worse it gets". If the harder you try, the worse it gets, then you should take another look at the methods you've been using. You've probably been tricked into trying to protect yourself against something that isn't dangerous, and this makes your fear worse over time.

How Can You Overcome The Anxiety Trick?

The thing that makes fears and phobias so persistent is that virtually anything you do to oppose, escape, or distract from the anxious feelings and thoughts will be turned against you, and make the anxiety a more persistent part of your life.

This is why people notice "the harder I try, the worse it gets". They're putting out fires with gasoline.

If you come to see that you've been putting out fires with gasoline, you may not have any idea what to do next. But the first step is always the same: put down the buckets. Stop throwing gasoline on that fire.

This is where the cognitive behavioral methods of desensitization and exposure come in. They're intended as methods by which you can practice with (not against) the symptoms, and become less sensitive to them. As you lose your fear of the symptoms, through this practice, that's when the symptoms will fade.

All too often, people get the idea that exposure means going to a place or situation where you're likely to get anxious, perhaps a highway or an elevator, and take a ride without getting anxious. That's not the point! The point is to actually go there and feel the anxiety, being sure to stay there and letting the anxiety leave first. This is what Claire Weekes called floating.

The way to disarm the Anxiety Trick is to increasingly spend time with anxiety, to expose yourself to the thoughts and sensations, and allow them to subside over time.

What can you do to make the experience of exposure more tolerable? You can use the AWARE steps as a general guide for how to conduct yourself while doing exposure. Always keep in mind that exposure is practice with fear, and do nothing to oppose, avoid, or distract from the fear during exposure.